Go Low

Learning Humility in a Hubristic Age

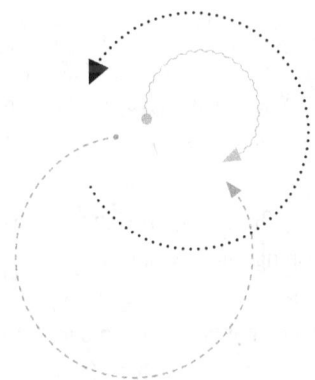

Dietrich Schindler

Go Low: Learning Humility in a Hubristic Age

Copyright © 2024 Dietrich Schindler.

All rights reserved. No part of this publication may be reproduced in any form without written permission from Book Villages, P.O. Box 64526, Colorado Springs, CO 80962. www.bookvillages.com

ISBN-13: 978-1-95756-627-6

Cover and Interior Design by Niddy Griddy Design, Inc.

Cover Photo © Adobe Stock

Unless otherwise indicated, all Scripture quotations are taken from the Holy Bible, New International Version (NIV), copyright ©1973, 1978, 1984, 2011 by International Bible Society. Other versions include: The New Living Translation (NLT) Copyright ©1996, 2004, 2007. Used by permission of Tyndale House Publishers, Inc., Carol Stream, Illinois 60188; The Holy Bible, English Standard Version® (ESV®) Copyright © 2001 by Crossway, a publishing ministry of Good News Publishers. All rights reserved; New International Reader's Version (NIRV) Copyright © 1995, 1996, 1998, 2014 by Biblica, Inc.® Used by permission. All rights reserved worldwide. New Revised Standard Version Bible: Anglicised Edition (NRSVA), copyright © 1989, 1995 the Division of Christian Education of the National Council of the Churches of Christ in the United States of America. Used by permission. All rights reserved; Amplified Bible (AMP) Copyright © 2015 by The Lockman Foundation, La Habra, CA 90631. All rights reserved; The Message (MSG) Copyright © 1993, 2002, 2018 by Eugene H. Peterson; New American Standard Bible®, Copyright © 1960, 1971, 1977, 1995, 2020 by The Lockman Foundation. All rights reserved; SAINT JOSEPH NEW CATHOLIC BIBLE® Copyright © 2019 by Catholic Book Publishing Corp. Used with permission. All rights reserved; The Holy Bible, International Children's Bible® Copyright© 1986, 1988, 1999, 2015 by Thomas Nelson. Used by permission; New King James Version®. Copyright © 1982 by Thomas Nelson. Used by permission. All rights reserved.

LCCN: 2024917250

Printed in the United States of America

1 2 3 4 5 6 7 8 / 28 27 26 25 24

Other Resources by Dietrich Schindler

Beyond Belief: Faith That Works

Profound: Twelve Questions That Will Grab Your Heart and Not Let Go

SHIFT: The Road to Level 5 Church Multiplication

The Jesus Model: Planting Churches the Jesus Way

Childrens Books:
The Tortoise and the Hair

Sweety-Peetie Speaks

Visit his blog and website:
dietrichschindler.com

Dedicated to

my dear friend and esteemed mentor

Mike Frans,

who like Jesus is *gentle and lowly,*

authentic and profound in all he is and does.

To be with Mike is to learn Jesus.

Table of Contents

Introduction

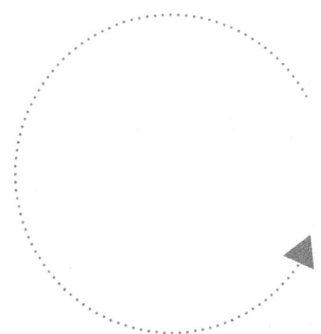

We've all witnessed it—the tears of those athletes who came in second or third. There they are, all three of them, standing on a staggered podium. The winner is exuberant as she, perched at the topmost step, thrusts up her gold medal in one hand and raises a bouquet of flowers in the other, beaming like the sun. Second and third place bravely display feigned happiness, for their tears betray their hearts. To the second-and-third place finishers, the only prize is the first prize.

While most of us have never participated in an Olympic sport, we all know what it's like to want that gold medal. It's important to us to be perceived as winners. Think about our last conversation when we began to get to know strangers. What was it that we shared with them about ourselves? Wasn't it something that had to do with our performance, our pedigree, or our position?

From early childhood, our parents praised us for accomplishing good things: eating with a spoon, taking our first step, or using the potty. Later, we learned that the degree of our acceptance by others varies based on the first four letters of the alphabet as seen on our report cards. From parents to professors to peers, the message is loud, and it is clear—losers finish last. Don't be a loser. If you want to get ahead in life, then be an achiever!

9

This achieving mentality spills over into the realm of religion. We perceive much of spirituality as based on being a good person; God is looking for moral winners. Losers need not apply. God is like our parents; He wants us to be high achievers.

The goal of religious people is to get to where God is, which is in heaven. Heaven is the place of ultimate good and happiness. It is the highest step on the podium. We imagine the route we need to take to get to God is akin to a ladder of morality; it begins below with rungs denoting badness and ends at the top near God and heaven with rungs denoting goodness. At the bottom are our axe murderers and heroin dealers. At the top are Mother Teresa and Opie. God is standing at the top of our ladder, cheering us on as we step up toward Him, His arms outstretched. He is not lifting a finger. It's all on us. Our job is to be winners, to be morally the best people we can be, so that ultimately God will be impressed, much like the judges at the Olympics. Thus, we spend our days ascending the ladder, hoping to supplant our vileness with goodness and thereby make progress in reaching the pinnacle. The summit is our goal. But to get to the top, we need to be top.

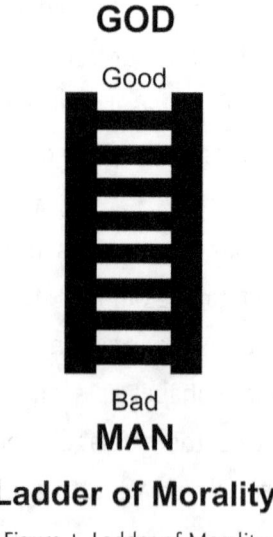

GOD

Good

Bad

MAN

Ladder of Morality

Figure 1. Ladder of Morality

Most religions with an earning-based foundation have the ladder of morality as their presupposition. But when we open our Bibles, we discover a different outlook. We read passages like:

Indeed, there is no one on earth who is righteous, no one who does what is right and never sins. (Ecclesiastes 7:20)

If we claim to be without sin, we deceive ourselves and the truth is not in us. (1 John 1:8)

Everyone has sinned. No one measures up to God's glory. (Romans 3:23, NIRV)

Such words wreak havoc with our perception of climbing the ladder of morality to get to God. This is not good news for Mother Teresa or for Opie. For it is not the rungs of the ladder that are pivotal, but the side rails. More paradoxical than contradictory, we are able to conduct ourselves both nobly and ignobly in one action. Or, sometimes, we do good things but with underlying bad motives.[1]

Even in our best moments, when we're outshining the competition, we fall short of the gold standard of absolute goodness. Some readers will balk at that last statement. They will want to justify their goodness at times by appealing to the competition: "But compared to Bob or Nancy, I'm doing pretty well." Often, the Bobs and the Nancys are those poor souls who we judge to be beneath us. Rarely, if ever, do we compare ourselves to those morally superior to us.

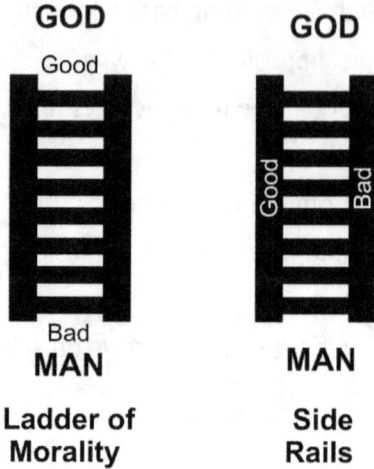

Ladder of Morality | **Side Rails**

Figure 2. Side Rails

We are shocked to discover that God does not grade on a curve. We continue to riffle back and forth in our Bibles for any kind of hope for the morally bankrupt, which is what we are. Then we find it—eureka! There is indeed an up and a down in the Bible! But the categories are contrarian. The up is not goodness but a bad thing, which we refer to as pride. And the down is not a bad thing but a virtue, which we label humility.

The Contrarian Ladder

Figure 3. The Contrarian Ladder

If God has a home, then it is in heaven. But if God has a second home here on earth, a kind of cottage on the lake, it is with folks who are humble.

For this is what the high and exalted One says—he who lives forever, whose name is holy: "I live in a high and holy place, but also with the one who is contrite and lowly in spirit, to revive the spirit of the lowly and to revive the heart of the contrite." (Isaiah 57:15)

These are the ones I look on with favor: those who are humble and contrite in spirit, and who tremble at my word. (Isaiah 66:2)

God is contrarian in what He loves and favors. He bypasses those who are full of themselves and moves in with those who are humble and have a proper estimation of reality and thus of themselves.

Christianity tells us that we do not ascend to God, but that God condescends, comes down, and descends the ladder to get to us. He would love to come to everyone, but alas, most are too preoccupied with themselves and their attempts at self-extension to even allow God into their lives. The baffling truth is this: God descends the ladder to step into the lives of those who are humble.[2]

Before we get to a heavenly home, God wants to be at home with us now.

My wife and I have recently moved from Germany, where we had lived for thirty-seven years, to a suburb of Chicago. We are literally living in her folks' basement. (We hope to be on the cusp of a new social movement—children in their sixties moving back to live with their parents in their basement.) We are beginning to converse about what it would mean to have our own place. We talk about many different features, like one-story, two-story, two bedrooms, four bedrooms, no basement, with basement, big lawn, small lawn, walk-in closet, or a man cave.

When God thinks about a living space, does He have you in mind?

After trust in Jesus Christ as our salvation, the only other feature He is really interested in is that of a humble heart. Would you consider yourself to be a humble person? What if we went on a journey together to learn to be God's kind of people in everyday life? What if we discovered how pernicious pride is and how it has infiltrated much of who we have become? And what if we had a way out? A better way? A path choked full of unexpected delight— the path of humble living where God feels right at home?

I invite you to join me on a journey to *Go Low*.

Section One:
With Pride as Our Guide

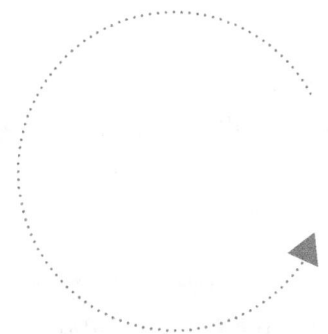

Exploring the strange new world of another country, cross-cultural missionaries have often needed trusted guides to help them understand their surroundings. Books, documentaries, and testimonies of people who have lived in their adopted land are helpful resources. But nothing compares to a national taking foreigners under her wing and helping them navigate language, customs, history, and geography. In like manner, what better guide to explore the land of pride than Pride itself?

The essence of humility is illuminated by the shadows cast by its opposite—pride. To understand what humility is, it is important to take ample time to reflect on what it is not. In securing Pride as our guide, we will be reminded that our scout is not external to us but resident within our souls. He has always been with us, sometimes nudging but often cajoling us to immerse ourselves in his world.

As we shall see, our guide is not neutral, but utterly enthusiastic about the world he inhabits. Our guide Pride is, after all, the best advertisement for desiring to live in his country. It is the land of opportunity, where the sky is the limit and nothing is forbidden. In the land of pride, impulses and feelings rule its people. "It can't be wrong if it feels so right" is stamped on the coinage. In the land of pride, living for today, the present tense,

15

trumps past and future tenses. It is a land free of such pesky restraints as shame and guilt. Becoming conversant in this new culture starts with rejecting those moral handcuffs that inhibit personal happiness—for happiness can only be attained, says our guide, as we jettison that which makes us sad, angry, depressed, and moody. There are morals, but they are relative to our own sense of well-being. In the land of pride, people are loved and valued conditionally—as they serve to feed our hunger for personal fulfillment.

Our guide is winsome, persuasive, suave, and entertaining. He will leave us wondering how in the world we would want to live in any other world than that which he inhabits. As he navigates us through the terrain of the land of pride, we will often have a sense of déjà vu; this terrain feels familiar as if we have lived here before. Indeed, we have. The land of pride is not a foreign country. It has been our homeland.

Chapter 1

Frisky

"In his blue gardens men and girls came and went like moths among the whisperings and the champagne and the stars."
F. Scott Fitzgerald[1]

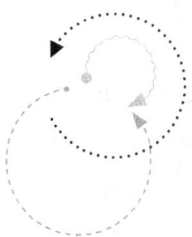

Have you ever experienced something so gloriously joyous that you couldn't stop laughing? As a boy growing up in a blue-collar, middle-class home, I remember such times of exquisite laughter.

As a hardworking electrician, when my dad wasn't bending pipes, wiring houses, or troubleshooting problems in a foundry, he was doing side jobs. When he wasn't earning a little extra to pay for our fishing adventures, he would be out in his shop working. My brother and I were his apprentices. It seemed like we were always working. It felt like we never had a time clock to punch out. I grew to regret that I wasn't free to join my friends at play because my jobs weren't yet finished.

Sundays were the days we stopped working; even my German father stopped. On rare Sunday afternoons, after having a nap and enjoying *Kaffee und Kuchen*, my younger brother and I would play on the family room floor with our plastic soldiers as we built forts with wooden blocks and tried to knock down each other's fortress with marbles catapulted.

17

Sometimes, out of the blue, Pop would swoop down on us and begin to wrestle with us. He would be on the floor, and in a flash, we would be on him. Up and down we went, rolling over and over. The laughter was so raucous—from all three of us—that I remember needing to cough uncontrollably. We had tears in our eyes; it was so much fun. This was pure, unexpected joy. And it was frisky.

Friskiness is playfulness. Kittens tumbling about on each other, Keith Jarrett improvising, and a courting couple walking side by side are playful. Friskiness is frolicsome, uninhibited, and sportive joy.

Friskiness in and of itself is neutral. Yet when it comes into contact with an overestimation of itself, it can turn bad, like lettuce left too long in the refrigerator. In this regard, playfulness becomes the gateway to pride.

In the 1990s, my wife, Jan, and I planted a church in Mannheim, Germany. By the grace of God, we saw many people come to know Jesus Christ as their joy and the captain of their lives. Young families and students became the core of our fellowship.

Along with reaching new people with the gospel, issues needed to be addressed in the lives of new believers. I remember a lovely young student asking to see me one day. She was wrestling with something and sought my counsel. Tammy (not her real name) loved to dance and would sometimes go to bars with her girlfriends. Her question to me was, "Is it wrong to flirt with guys?" Tammy was very attractive and enjoyed the sport of teasing and leading men on. In doing so, she told me she meant no harm and would not go to bed with them. She was exploring her own desirability and testing her market value. My answer to her was, "Tammy, though you mean no harm, the casual manner in which you flirt with men arouses something in them that gives way to hope. That hope is seeing you in bed with them." She got the message and adjusted her behavior. Friskiness is an open door to more.

Lust or desire for things seen and craved is what the Apostle John called worldliness. "For everything in the world—the lust of the flesh, the lust of the eyes, and the pride of life—comes not from the Father but from the world. The world and its desires pass away, but whoever does the will of God lives forever" (1 John 2:16-17). In other words, John was exposing the fallacy of materialism, which is the attachment of our affections to those things that attract us that are both temporal and doomed to decay. What we gaze upon, dream about, and allow our thoughts to carousel around affects our affections.

Figure 4. Ship of Fools by Hieronymus Bosch
(Used by permission.)

Hieronymus Bosch, a Dutch painter, showed us what happens when frivolity tethered to self ripens. Around 1500, Bosch painted a picture of a ship loaded with people who were living it up. Men and women are seen in festive gaiety, eating sumptuous food and drinking copious amounts of expensive wine. In total disregard for safety, two naked men have gone overboard and, in spite of being in danger of drowning, seem unaffected. The lute and the bowl of cherries suggest sexual arousal. In the middle of the picture, a pancake is suspended from a mast without a sail. People are trying to eat it. The pancake resembles the host of the Lord's Supper. These are obviously people who have a voracious hunger for food while ignoring the necessities of existence. Instead of an oar that would steer the ship, we see a giant wooden spoon. The ship is far from shore and in great danger, yet those on board are, in their frivolity, oblivious to their impending doom. It is such an absurd scene that even a court jester has turned his back on the festive crowd.

Bosch was granting us a glimpse of those who have substituted baser appetites for a life lived in reverence to God. These people are obviously delusional. Having lost their internal compass, they have become unmoored; in their journey through life, they are terribly lost. An owl, often a symbol of wisdom, is seen frowning. These are not wise people. The painting is a commentary on society then and now. Fittingly, Bosch titled his painting *Ship of Fools*.

Psalm 10 is an appropriate commentary on the carousing going on in Bosch's painting.

> He boasts about the cravings of his heart; he blesses the greedy and reviles the Lord. In his pride the wicked man does not seek him; in all his thoughts there is no room for God. His ways are always prosperous; your laws are rejected by him; he sneers at all his enemies. He says to himself, "Nothing will ever shake me." He swears, "No one will ever do me harm." (Psalm 10:3-6)

Contemporary society balks at what Bosch was communicating: a life lived hedonistically, without God at its center, is doomed. Philosopher and theologian Cornelius Plantinga captured for us the tone of our age.

To them [i.e., those who reject God and a universe ruled by Him], the proposal that we ought to worship someone who is better than we are, that we ought to study this person's will and then bend our lives to it, that we ought to confess our failures and assign life's blessings to him—to them, the notion that we ought to take this posture toward anybody else at all is humiliatingly undemocratic, an offense to human dignity and pride.[2]

The book of Proverbs in the Old Testament, words of wisdom from sages of old, has much to say about the fool and his folly. "Folly brings joy to one who has no sense" (Proverbs 15:21). The empty-headed and the wrongheaded are senseless; "folly is fun," they say as they chase after vanities, empty as misty vapor.

As innocuous as excitability may seem, when pride enters the picture, friskiness changes hue. This is because pride is, at its core, a parasite, attaching itself to something beautiful, only to misuse it for darker pursuits. Pride is always flirting with someone or something.

What is pride? Pride is both an overestimation and an underestimation. Pride overestimates the importance of self while underestimating the importance (and position) of God and other people. In financial terms, pride is embezzlement—taking from others what rightfully belongs to them for the sake of personal enrichment.

As such, pride is firstly an affront against the person and the position of God. "He mocks proud mockers" (Proverbs 3:34). "God opposes the proud" (1 Peter 5:5). Why? Because the prideful person has opposed God in his thoughts, deeds, feelings, and desires. In seeking to rise above God and His designs for humans, flourishing the self-inflated person becomes their own god—the first and last resort of what it means to be a fully satisfied human being. Pride is placing so much value on ourselves that we disregard God and His purpose for us.

Perhaps a passage in the book of Job was a seedbed for Bosch's painting. "Though the pride of the godless person reaches to the heavens and his head touches the clouds, he will perish forever, like his own dung; those who have seen him will say, 'Where is he?'" (Job 20:6-7). Even the fool of fools, the jester himself, seems to agree with this assessment of the proud at play.

What Plantinga did in outlining the doctrine of sin is true of pride, which is sin's taproot. "All sin has first and finally a Godward force. Let us say that a sin is any act—any thought, desire, emotion, word, or deed—or its particular absence, that displeases God and deserves blame. . . . Sin is a culpable and personal affront to a personal God."[3]

The human heart is only so large as to be able to contain one center. That center can either be self or God. The two cannot coexist. One or the other must go because it is at the very center of our hearts that dominion becomes fixed. Our souls are then regulated either by self-interest or by God-interest.

Cream Puff!

Pride is the opposite of humility. The Latin word for pride is *superbia*, which means "above." Superbia is essentially the elevation of oneself above others. Pride is an expression of inflation—an overextended view of one's self-importance. More people live in *superbia* than in suburbia.

Among pastries, pride is the cream puff of anti-virtues. The Apostle Paul described his opponents in the Corinthian church as "arrogant" or "full of pride," using the Greek word *physio*, which means "full of hot air" (1 Corinthians 4:18). We instinctively know what he meant by this. Like a mighty popover that is essentially an empty shell of dough, the proud person distorts reality, making himself appear more important than he truly is, like a five-foot four-inch man looking over the heads of NBA centers.

We are living in inflationary times, not only monetarily but, more importantly, persona-wise. TikTok, a plethora of influencers, mobbing at schools, inflated résumés, politicians falsely citing universities they never attended or a company for which they never worked, all crave for the public to see them not as they are, but as they want to be perceived. Image has trumped substance. The sin of pride is everywhere, even within us. People want others to perceive them as six foot seven when they are an underwhelming five foot four.

Both pride and humility have the same source. It is the self, the soul. We human beings, made in the image of God, our Creator, have what animals do not have—a soul. Our soul, who we truly are, is a nonmaterial substance. We do not have souls; we are souls. We are souls contained in bodies that are decaying and will one day die. Death is the separation of the soul from the body. The soul is personhood; it is what we think, feel, and will; it is the center of discernment and judgment.

Our souls are like GPS systems in our cars; they seek calibration. When they are calibrated, what we think, do, and feel emanates from our synced self. The path to soul calibration is one of two routes: either our souls orient toward themselves or they orient toward God, who is outside of ourselves. The taproot of our inner being is either ourselves or God.

Sometimes it is helpful to envision what life is like in either being centered on self or being centered on God.

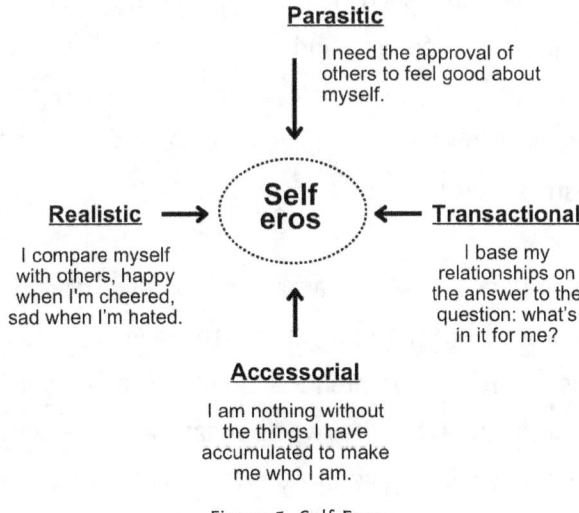

Figure 5. Self-Eros

Having an overestimation of oneself is our definition of pride. Eros is at the core of pride. Instead of cultivating a steady urge for God to be at the center of our lives, we are driven by the pursuit of personal happiness. All erotic love is based upon attraction, which, in turn, emanates from the self-seeking to be pleasured. Eros is often touted as love, but in truth, it is a cheap imitation of love, and it is an offshoot of agape. When we live for pleasure, people become objects that we use to engineer our happiness. What we get as a result is always gnawing dissatisfaction and a sense of emptiness. Much anger and bodily harm in this world are the fruit of eros, both fulfilled and unfulfilled—leaving behind unending frustration that lashes out with words, fists, and even guns.

Lewis Smedes wrote of the frustration that eros inevitably delivers to our doorstep.

> Erotic love is the root of irritability because it is personal power generated by personal need. We reach out and strive for anything that promises to satisfy our deep desires to be complete human beings. Where do we get the idea that there must be more to life than we have found? Why do we never stop dreaming of a full life? Why are we never satisfied? The answer is *eros*. Eros is the restless human drive for happiness and completeness. The urge comes from the abyss of our souls. At its deepest, it is the urge for God, profoundly and memorably expressed in Augustine's confession, "Our hearts are restless until they find their rest in thee."[4]

Notice in Figure 5 how the arrows are pointed inward toward the self. The outer world of the prideful self, the environment around it, is what it needs to feed upon to produce its self-worth. We will see that the soul indeed needs an anchor to live abundantly. But when that anchor is circumstance, people, image projection, opinion, or materialism—all weak in nature—that anchor will be ripped away, leaving us adrift like the revelers in Bosch's painting.

Pride is an overestimation of self at the cost of an underestimation of who God is. Pride was the fuse that, once lit, caused our first parents to both explode and implode. All other sins were born out of the original sin of pride.

Martin Luther coined a Latin term that well fits with what we are exploring: *incurvitus in se,* translated as "curved inward on oneself."[5] When a person turns away from God as his orientation, all he has left is himself. The soul of the person curved into himself becomes its sole authority in living, not God. The soul at the center, divorced from God, is the origin of pride.

In Greek mythology, we learn that Hybris was the daughter of father Nyx (from which we derive the word *night*) and mother Erebus (*darkness*). Roman mythology names her Petulantia, from which we derive *petulant*—boastful. In contemporary usage, hybris is that person who is full of themselves, often reflected in boasting. This is what we mean when we say someone is proud.

The Metastasis of Pride

We go to our annual checkup suspecting all will go well. After our doctor has run his tests, he requests us to come in for a summary consultation. The look on his face awakens in us a feeling of foreboding. *Something is not right,* shoots up through our consciousness. And we are correct in what we sense. Somberly, our physician tells us that we have cancer, and that it is both pathological and aggressive. From the base of our cancer cells, other death-carrying cells have broken away and are being transported to other parts of our body. Our kidneys, liver, and bladder have been affected. The cancer has spread, and it has metastasized. The end of our life is now measured not in years but in weeks and days.

Pride is a cancer that spreads throughout our souls. We do well to have an MRI and a CAT scan done on the cancer of pride. What are the signs that it has spread out and affected every part of who we are as persons?

My projection of myself is better than the real me.

Social scientists tell us that we lie an average of six times per day.[6] In lying, we project an image of ourselves that is not commensurate with reality. Why do we do this? Because we fear what people might think of us if they knew our true selves. And because we fear their rejection, we live in a world of artificiality; our own personal version of *The Truman Show*. Image becomes everything. Thus, it is important that people do *not* know the real me, but just an embellishment of who I am. Should we doubt this, all we need to do is visit an online dating site. Self-promotion and image projection are mutations of the cancer of pride that has settled securely in our hearts, making us smaller and ultimately lonelier than we had anticipated.

Only by comparing myself with others and thereby feeling superior do I feel good about myself.

Schadenfreude is the German term for the glee that we feel at the stumbling of others. Schadenfreude (gloating) is now a widely used term in American society. We prop ourselves up by comparing ourselves to those less beautiful, less fortunate, less successful, and less healthy than we are. To be us, we need others to be weak, for therein we garner our (perceived) strength.

What happens, in fact, is that there are boatloads of people who, when we compare ourselves to them, are way ahead of us. They are *more*—beautiful, youthful, wealthy, healthy, intelligent, and well-situated. Comparison is a game that we will always lose. It will ultimately lead to despair and depression, or worse.

I am what I have accomplished.

Pride has metastasized when we reduce personal worth to performance. It is instructive to note that in the bloodline of Cain in Genesis, those who, like Cain, rejected God's rule over them turned to grand schemes to underscore their sense of well-being.

They said to each other, "Come, let's make bricks and bake them thoroughly." They used brick instead of stone, and tar for mortar. Then they said, "Come, let us build ourselves a city, with a tower that reaches to the heavens, so that we may make a name for ourselves; otherwise we will be scattered over the face of the whole earth" (Genesis 11:3-4).

Making a name for themselves, having a reputation, and being perceived as successful were all performance-based. The city with a tower reaching to the heavens was their way of saying, "I accomplish, therefore I am." How frail is that! All that needs to happen is an economic downturn, a debilitating sickness, or a pink slip to knock us out of the game and render us incapable of performing.

God knows that performance is the idol of choice for many of us. We bow down to the god of success and worship it, for we become what we worship. How does the true God respond to success-worship? Like in the Genesis account, He frustrates our efforts. For He will not allow us to be reduced to our accomplishments.

I know what's best for me.
When we take life into our own hands, we make God small. Only one person can be in the driver's seat. If it is us, then it cannot be God. Sarai and Abram were the ages of grandma and grandpa when God told them they would have a son from whom God would raise up a great nation. Sarai got impatient. When a person gets impatient, she generally gets creative. Impatient Sarai took her destiny into her own hands, and "so she said to Abram, 'The LORD has kept me from having children. Go, sleep with my slave; perhaps I can build a family through her'" (Genesis 16:2).

Like the builders of the tower of Babel, Sarai thought she knew what was best for her and her husband. Instead of relying on God and His promises, Sarai and Abram succumbed to expediency. We see the cancer spreading, effectively pushing God to the perimeter of their lives, making Him relevant only when they perceive Him as being relevant to them to help them get ahead.

Fast-forward to the next two generations, and we discover Laban and Jacob reheating the sin of Sarai to fit their own "I know what's best for me" scenarios. Laban deceived Jacob by giving him his daughter Leah as a wife rather than the promised beauty, Rachel. Jacob said, "I served you for Rachel, didn't I? Why have you deceived me?" (Genesis 29:25). Jacob turned the tables on his father-in-law by stealthily leaving town. When Laban caught up with Jacob and his entourage of wives, children, servants, and wealth, he said, "What have you done? You've deceived me, and you've carried off my daughters like captives in war. Why did you run off secretly and deceive me? Why didn't you tell me, so I could send you away with joy and singing to the music of timbrels and harps?" (Genesis 31:26-27).

Living life according to the maxim "I know what is best for me" is a burden that will ultimately crush us. Who better to reflect on the destructive weight of living narcissistically than the great Saint Augustine? Before he gave his life to follow Christ at the age of thirty-two, Augustine was the Hugh Hefner of his society. This is what he said of that time of his life while living excessively,

> I could not distinguish the clear light of true love from the murk of lust. Love and lust together seethed within me. In my tender youth, they swept me away over the precipice of my body's appetites and plunged me into the whirlpool of sin. More and more I angered you, unawares. For I had been deafened by the clank of my chains, the fetters of death which were my due to punish the pride in my soul. . . . I went on my way, farther and farther from you, proud in my distress and restless in fatigue, sowing more and more seeds whose only crop was grief.[7]

I am my sexual orientation.

Once upon a time, biology determined sexuality. The chromosomes in our DNA were self-evident, allowing us to be called either a boy or a girl. Contemporary society is now rejecting this foundational truth, referring to it as a form of slavery. On the throne of self, where eros is king, we can now free ourselves from our biological "bondage" and determine not only with whom we can be sexually active but also choose our gender at will.

The poster child for transgenderism is Caitlyn Jenner, who used to be known as Olympic medalist Bruce Jenner. Jenner publicly declared his identity as a female in an interview conducted by Diane Sawyer of ABC News in April 2015. In his (or her) own words, this is what Jenner said:

I would say I've always been very confused with my gender identity since I was this big. I tried to explain it, because I've had all my kids sitting in that chair and I've tried to explain it to them this way. God's looking down, making little Bruce, okay? He's looking down. He says,

"Okay, what are we going to do with this one?" Make him a smart kid, very determined. And he gave me all of these wonderful qualities. And at the end, when He's just finishing, He goes, "Wait a second, we've gotta give him something. Everybody has stuff in their life that they have to deal with, you know? What are we gonna give him?" God looks down and chuckles a little bit and goes, "Hey, let's give him the soul of a female, and let's see how he deals with that." You know? So here I am stuck. And I hate the words "girl stuck in a guy's body"; I hate that terminology.[8]

Jenner's testimony flies in the face of *imago dei*, that he was made in God's image. Biblically speaking, identity is inheritance, not production. When God made humanity, He gifted us with His stamp of maleness or femaleness. To come to the point of rejecting who God made us to be is the height of rebellion or the logical conclusion to an eros-directed self.

Historian Carl Trueman referred to the end result of choosing one's own gender as highly unstable.

If I am whoever I think I am and if my inward sense of psychological well-being is my only moral imperative, then the imposition of external, prior, or static categories is nothing other than an act of imperialism, an attempt to restrict my freedom or to make me inauthentic. Nietzsche saw this in the nineteenth century. At the same time, Karl Marx and Charles Darwin were also stripping nature of its given metaphysical authority. In this context, transgenderism is merely the latest iteration of self-creation that becomes necessary in the wake of decreation.[9]

However, transgenderism is the outgrowth of a more deep-seated problem. Mimicking God, transgender people want to be in charge of their own creation. But it's never ex nihilo, out of nothing, as Genesis tells us God's creation was. But in wanting to improve upon what God has given, they deform themselves and, in so doing, descend deeper down into the spiral of despair. Changing the form of her body never really addressed the ache in her soul. With pride as her guide, she supplanted the true Creator and manufactured a new false self. And this new image has the vigorous power to enslave and destroy.

In The Great Gatsby, Nick Carraway is our guide to a world of revelry, lively jazz bands, and excessive alcohol consumption in the 1920s when alcohol was prohibited by law; glamorous people of great wealth with greater arrogance set the scene for us. On Long Island in the village of West Egg, an opulent mansion is awash in light and gaiety till the early hours of the weekend. Multimillionaire Jay Gatsby presides over parties to which the rich and famous of Manhattan flock.

We learn that Jay is in love with Daisy, who is wrapped up in an unhappy marriage with Tom Buchanan, who is cheating on his wife by seeing Myrtle, the homely wife of George Wilson. While he was in the army, Gatsby met Daisy before she was married and fell in love with her. Five years later, he learns that she and Tom are living on Long Island.

Gatsby purchases a mansion on the water across the bay on which the Buchanans live. Every night, he gazes over the bay to peer at the green light emanating from Daisy's home.

Nick Carraway is a bond broker in Manhattan and a neighbor to Gatsby. When Gatsby learns that Nick is Daisy's cousin, he begins to spend much of his time with him. The opulent parties at Gatsby's villa, we learn, are only a pretense to lure Tom and Daisy to his compound. Lurking in the shadows and on the fringe of hundreds of guests partying, Gatsby pursues Daisy.

We begin to peek behind the curtain. Nick says of Gatsby,

He might have despised himself, for he had certainly taken her under false pretenses. I don't mean that he had traded on his phantom millions, but he had deliberately given Daisy a sense of security; he let her believe that he was a person from much the same strata as herself—that he was fully able to take care of her. As a matter of fact, he had no such facilities—he had no comfortable family standing behind him, and he was liable at the whim of an impersonal government to be blown anywhere about the world.[10]

In the end, we learn of where hybris has taken this frisky collage of unhappy people feigning mirth. Myrtle is run over by Daisy driving Gatsby's car and dies. In a jealous rage, Tom Buchanan shoots Jay Gatsby in his swimming pool, after which he pulls the trigger against his own temple.

Gatsby believed in the green light, the orgiastic future that year by year recedes before us. It eluded us then, but that's no matter— tomorrow we will run faster, stretch out our arms farther. . . . And one fine morning—

So we beat on, boats against the current, borne back ceaselessly into the past."[11]

Going Deeper

Questions are *quests* toward deeper insight and better application. Individually or as a group, the following questions invite you to wade into greater depth of understanding.

- Where have you experienced friskiness (playfulness) in your life as a gateway to greater self-absorption?
- The definition of pride is both an overestimation of one's self-importance and underestimation of God's ultimate importance. Think of yesterday. Where did you overestimate yourself, and where did you underestimate God?
- In looking at Figure 5 "Self-Eros," which of the four descriptions (parasitic, transactional, accessorial, realistic) has been most dominant in your life? Give examples.
- Review the descriptors of "The Metastasis of Pride." Which ones ring true for you?
- Which of the following lies have you told in the past week? "You look great!" "I'm fine." "I didn't do anything wrong." "It's not about you."
- What is one insight that you gained from this chapter? Spend ten minutes thinking about it more deeply.

Chapter 2

Lost

"I know no way of discounting the doctrine that when you take something you want, and damn the consequences, then you had better be ready to accept whatever consequences ensue."
WALLACE STEGNER[1]

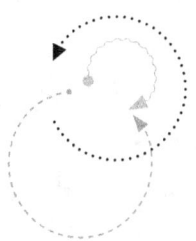

At the end of our eight-year church-planting adventure in Kaiserslautern, Germany, the good folks of the fellowship there gave Jan and me a lovely goodbye gift. It was a weekend in an upscale hotel deep in the Palatine Forest in southwestern Germany, all expenses paid. *How wonderful,* we thought.

Indeed, it was a very nice hotel with a good German restaurant. What to do? We discovered that the reception desk had maps of trails of various lengths that one could traverse. All were well marked and indicated topography and length. We both like to hike, and this seemed like a fine way to spend a Saturday afternoon.

The beauty of the trees, the quietness of the forest, and the smell of fresh air were invigorating. As we walked and talked, we joked. I said to Jan, "I forgot to take breadcrumbs to leave along the path to find our way back." We laughed. But, very much like Hansel and Gretel, we got lost along the way. Was it the black-and-white poorly photocopied map, or was it a marker missed on a tree? We did not know. What we did know was that we were lost. At first, we made fun of the whole affair, conjuring up specious headlines in local newspapers: "Found After Three Days, Pastor and Wife Survive on Mushrooms and Roots."

But after several hours of twists and turns, feet getting weary and hearts heavy, fear began to creep up between us. "What if darkness sets upon us?" "Did you hear that? I think I heard a truck." We were truly at the end of our rope when we rounded a bend and saw, to our great relief, a group of men in the forest cutting down trees. They were able to show us where we were and how to get from where we were back to the hotel. We were saved. What a relief!

With Pride as our guide, we enter the forest via friskiness, but once in, we discover we are in over our heads. Pride is a guide without a sense of direction. In fact, should we follow him, we will ultimately lose our way, much as Jay Gatsby, Daisy, Tom, and Myrtle did.

Yet here we are on our journey in the land of self-absorption, with countless routes leading to personal self-fulfillment. We ourselves, guided by ourselves, are purely intending to find ourselves. All that matters in life is to be self-fulfilled. Which means what? We are not exactly sure, but we will die trying. On our map of the land of self-absorption, our markers all have eros—the love of self—over them. We have thus agreed on our destination: personal self-fulfillment, and now we are faced with many roads that will take us there.

But before we begin our journey toward greater self-fulfillment, we need to accumulate the right gear to help us get there. We will need good therapists, those well-trained folks who are warm, empathic, and genuine, whose job it is to shore up our fragile egos. They are the priests we go to when we want to better our lot in life. In their work to strengthen us, they have their own resources that they make available to us, such as self-help books, soothing music on the radio, and popular culture, which tells us, "We are here for you. Be the best of who you are. Your parents did it to you. Get rid of those who make you unhappy. You only go around once in life—grab for all the gusto you can. Get off my lawn!"

Not always being in the right mood on our journey to self-fulfillment, our doctors will provide us with the right kind of medication that will ensure that we will have the strength to carry on. Antidepressants are standard food. We will stock up on things that make us feel good: all new clothes, boats, shoes, and for husbands, anything found at Home Depot.

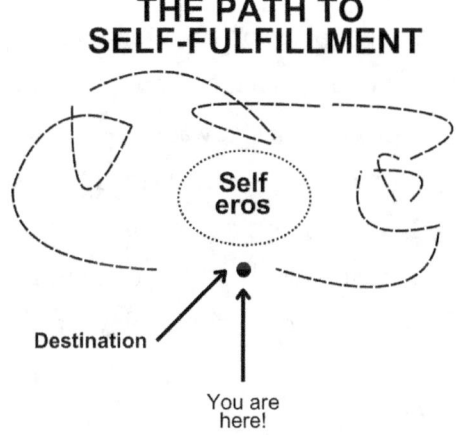

Figure 6. The Path to Self-Fulfillment

Our journey will be circular in nature. We will begin with ourselves and with the goal of finding ourselves. In the end, we will come back to where we started. There is no other destination. Let us begin.

Five Paths to Our Destination: Self-Fulfillment
The Path of Emotions
If our motivation for being self-fulfilled is to feel good about ourselves, we will likely take the path of feelings to get there. Instead of what is right, admirable, virtuous, or even what pleases God becoming our north star, we focus on how we feel about where we are at the moment. The path of emotion has no past and future tense. The hedonism of which we speak emphasizes that it is only the present moment that counts. As songwriter Barbara Mandrell sings, "How can it be wrong (when it feels so right)."[2]

Truth and morality collapse into this present moment and how we feel. Social scientists have discerned a shift in the way Western society has come to where we are today. One hundred and thirty years ago, at the turn of the twentieth century, we shifted away from character to personality as the foundation for human flourishing. Character was something to be learned and practiced; private desires took a back seat to what was best for those around us. Historian Warren Susman conveyed to us the descriptives used to showcase a culture based on character. They were "citizenship, duty, democracy, work, building, golden deeds, outdoor life, conquest, honor, reputation, morals, manners, integrity, and above all, manhood."[3] Such character was largely based upon the belief that there was a higher moral law that governed all people to which we were obliged. Then, around 1890, a change began to take place. Susman wrote the adjectives most commonly used to describe personality became "fascinating, stunning, attractive, magnetic, glowing, masterful, creative, dominant, and forceful."[4]

> None of these words could easily be used to describe someone's character. Character is not stunning, fascinating, or creative. . . . Attention was shifting from moral virtues, which needed to be cultivated, to the image, which needed to be fashioned. It was a shift away from the invisible moral intentions toward the attempt to make ourselves appealing to others, away from what we actually are and toward refining our performance before a public that mostly judges the exterior.[5]

Being in touch with our feelings and expressing them has seemingly become a national obsession. "People get fascinated with how they feel—and with how they feel about how they feel. In such a culture and the throes of such fascination, the self exists to be explored, indulged, and expressed but not disciplined or restrained."[6]

Emphasizing how we feel puts us on unsure footing if we grant our emotions too much authority. Feelings come and go. Are we to change direction purely based on whether we got a good eight hours of sleep last night or had enough caffeine to win the Preakness? There is, after all, reality to consider. Reality will manage to trump feelings. Feeling good when behind the wheel passing a car on a secondary road at a high rate of speed will alter quickly when we discover a ten-ton semitrailer barreling toward us in the opposite lane. Reality may hurt our feelings (and our bodies). Why? Because reality is the way things are, whereas feelings are what we want them to be.

The Path of Self-Reliance

Somebody needs to be in control of our journey toward self-fulfillment, and it might as well be us. After all, who better to know what suits us and brings us happiness than we ourselves? We place ourselves squarely in the driver's seat. We are running the show.

Self-actualization is the term psychologists have given to describe our reliance on ourselves. According to current philosophy, self-actualization is the individualization of the self. There are no other dominant means of informing our decision-making, lovemaking, career-seeking, or Christmas shopping than us. We want to be true to ourselves. If push comes to shove, we will lean on ourselves to get us out of tight circumstances or make the best of our opportunities.

Another term for this is the broadly used phrase *spirituality*. Oprah Winfrey has dedicated her considerable resources to fostering spirituality among her listeners. Under the heading "What I Know for Sure," Oprah wrote,

Spirituality for me is recognizing that I am connected to the energy of all creation, that I am a part of it—and it is always a part of me. Whatever label or word we use to describe *it* doesn't matter. Words are completely inadequate.

Spirituality is not religion. You can be spiritual and not have a religious context. The opposite is true too: You can be very religious with no spiritual dimension, just doctrine.

Spirituality isn't something I believe in. It is what and who I am: a spiritual being having a human experience, as the French philosopher and priest Pierre Teilhard de Chardin profoundly said.

Knowing this has made all the difference. It allows me to live fearlessly. And to make manifest the purpose of my creation. And I will be bold enough to say I know for sure it's the greatest discovery of life: to recognize that there's more than your body and your mind.

For several years in the 1990s, I did a segment on my show called "Remembering Your Spirit"—in spite of being ridiculed in the press for it and getting pushback from some viewers who weren't willing to accept the message that there's more to our lives than our five senses reveal.

Over the years, I've continued to find new ways of introducing the concept of spirit to a broad audience. This magazine is one of them—the mission being to help people find their best life, a life that acknowledges mind, body, and spirit.

Claiming my own spiritual depths and encouraging others to recognize the fullness of their potential through spiritual connection is my greatest purpose and calling.[7]

What, in the eyes of Oprah, is spirituality? In the classical meaning "of the Spirit of God" in the Christian tradition, it is not. Her spirituality is severed from a personal God and has mutated into a cosmic force that is seemingly behind everything. To get in touch with this force and harness it for personal satisfaction is what Oprah means by spirituality. Oprah is on the path of self-reliance. She is harnessing cosmic energy to make her life better. Self-fulfillment is her goal.

David Wells gave us a sobering assessment of what Oprah's philosophy of life entails and the shortcomings of life lived in self-actualization and the individualization of the self.

> At the center stands the belief that others are the threat to our own reality. Thus the ethic of self-actualization "assigns ultimate moral priority to the self, over and society" so that "any action governed by social convention rather than individual preference . . . is tantamount to self-violation" [quoting John Rice]. Even one's deepest commitments, such as to one's spouse, children, friends, and faith, as well as one's obligations to institutions and society, all become matters of negotiation lest they become encumbrances to being more personally satisfied.[8]

To be one's first and last frame of reference in living life is also called being our own god. The self has become a deity, sitting on the throne and ruling benevolently over us, but never contradictory to what we believe is true for us. Our god is handmade, looking a lot like the person in whom it dwells. As such, we, as gods, are simply a projection of ourselves but a little bit bigger and not fraught with the foibles that bother us and others. Cornelius Plantinga went even deeper.

> A proud person tries to reinvent reality. He tries to redraw the borders of human behavior to suit himself, displacing God as the Lord and boundary keeper of life. At bottom, the fool is out of touch with reality. For, of course, our wills are not sovereign. We are not really our own centers, anchors, or lawgivers. We have not made ourselves, cannot keep ourselves, cannot ultimately oblige or forgive ourselves. The image of ourselves as center of the world is fantasy.[9]

If this path does not suit us, perhaps we should seek out another one.

The Path of Comparison

On this path toward greater self-fulfillment, we will be instinctively looking over our shoulders, trying to keep up with the Joneses. Another description of this pathway could be "The Path of Things." Our motto is: the more we have, the better off we are. It is the classic doctrine of materialism; my boat, my house, my career, my bank account, my Chihuahua are what matter most in living abundantly.

When the devil sought to upend Jesus, he enticed Him with the prospect of wealth. "Again, the devil took him to a very high mountain and showed him all the kingdoms of the world and their splendor. 'All this I will give you,' he said, 'if you will bow down and worship me'" (Matthew 4:8–9).

According to *Forbes* magazine, most people would have jumped at the devil's offer.

> Life in the 21st century is a fast paced, consumer oriented experience where media surrounds us at all times enforcing the idea that happiness is a matter of buying the perfect house, driving the best car, wearing the trendiest clothes and posting status updates on the latest high tech devices. Everywhere we look we are inundated with the same message: "BUY, BUY, BUY your way to happiness!"[10]

Gordon Gekko agreed. In the film *Wall Street*, Gekko said, "Greed, for the lack of a better word, is good. Greed is right; greed works. Greed clarifies, cuts through, and captures the essence of the evolutionary spirit. Greed, in all of its forms—greed for life, for money, for love, for knowledge—has marked the upward surge of mankind."[11]

There is a decided difference between possessing wealth and wealth possessing us. Gordon Gekko did not have riches; riches had him. We might refer to this as the downside of prosperity: obtaining monetary affluence and, in the process, being held captive by the very thing we supposed would give us freedom. If it is true that the prize we seek often leads to captivity, why do we still seek it?

Despite what some people tell us, money can indeed provide happiness. The woman who gets a raise is happier with her new salary than with her old level of income. The man who learns of an unexpected inheritance rejoices in his good fortune. Even little children, when handed a coin or two, will skip away in delight. The happiness that an increase in income or possessions affords is real. Money can generate happiness. But the kind of happiness that wealth generates is significantly distinct.

Material prosperity generates happiness, but it is a kind of happiness made up of inferior quality. For lack of a better word, it is mammon-based happiness predicated upon the size of a bank account, the second house on a beautiful lake, and the number of $100 bills in a wallet. Happiness brought on by things we acquire or experiences we have comes with a shelf life. Studies have shown that the effect a raise has on us lasts a whole ten days. On the eleventh day, we tend to say to ourselves, "I deserved that." Material things are essentially lifeless. What gives them power is the value that we invest in them. If we think them to be valuable assets, then, by some unknown magical power, they become what we believe. But our belief is illusionary. The emperor has no clothes.

The pursuit of mammon can actually be harmful. Affluenza is described as "a painful, contagious, socially transmitted condition of overload, debt, anxiety, and waste resulting from the dogged pursuit of more."[12] A few years ago, a teenager who, with his mother, fled to Mexico to avoid being indicted in the United States for manslaughter charges was said to have suffered from incoherency brought on by being spoiled with riches. The wealth that his parents gave him resulted in a superior sense of well-being; because he had it all, he could do it all—and get away with avoiding dire consequences. Money clearly befuddled this young man's thinking.

But the gravest danger in the pursuit of prosperity is demonic in nature. The devil connected the transmission of "all the kingdoms of the world and their splendor" with worship. Worship is submission to the will and power of someone or something greater than we are. Greed is submission to prosperity. Greed is demonic because it disavows God as the highest being in the universe, who is to be revered over all things.[13]

To be brutally honest, we really don't want wealth at the expense of health. Living for things will do bad things to our inner disposition. Our moods will be tethered to how the S&P 500 did today and how that has affected our pot of gold. We will end up being the kind of people other people would not like to have around: grumpy, moody, unpredictable, chronically discontent, and barren.

W. H. Auden's poem "September 1, 1939" encapsulates the mood that overcomes us when, with self-eros as our guide, we cling to gratuitous circumstances that make us happy:

Faces along the bar
Cling to their average day:
The lights must never go out,
The music must always play . . .
Lest we should see where we are,
Lost in a haunted wood,
Children afraid of the night
Who have never been happy or good.[14]

There has to be a better path to being self-fulfilled.

The Path of Atheism
We have hinted at it all along. It's time to acknowledge it. For many people, the best path to personal self-fulfillment is that of disavowing God in their lives. This makes sense. For *us* to be satisfied, we need

to be free individuals. But as long as there is a God who will hold us accountable for how we have lived and who we have ultimately trusted in life, we will feel inhibited. Bondage is another word for what we are thinking. We do not want to be people who are told what to do and who to believe in. A free person is thus a person free from God.

Our guide, Pride, is heavily into divorce. He wants those under his wings to divorce themselves from God as the Creator and Sustainer of the universe and thus our daily lives. The alternative is to marry themselves to themselves. They, and not God, become their most intimate source of fulfillment.

Oxford Professor Richard Dawkins, in his book *The God Delusion*, blatantly stated what many people harbor in their hearts: "There is something infantile in the presumption that somebody else has a responsibility to give your life meaning and point. . . . The truly adult view, by contrast, is that our life is as meaningful, as full and as wonderful as we choose to make it."[15]

"Only fools say in their hearts, 'There is no God'" (Psalm 14:1, NLT). The Bible is audacious in pronouncing atheists fools, including the learned Professor Dawkins. Atheism is theism in new clothing. The ultimate authority of what is truth and the one who has power over life and death is God. A person who has rejected the Judeo-Christian God as God sets themselves up as their own god.

As to Dawkins' criticism of believers in God being infantile, who is more infantile? The person who has no control over her birth and has no idea of when her life will end, or the One who is the author of our beginning and our ending? Dawkins seems to have succumbed to the twin children of pride: arrogance and presumption. Indeed, he is full of both.

The Path of Education

Socrates taught that the way to virtue is through the acquisition of knowledge. If men only knew what virtue was, they would want to become virtuous. Our age is not an age of seeking virtue (although it's sorely needed). It is an age of pursuing personal flourishing. Yet the pathway is the same as that for Socrates—knowledge.

The more we know, the better off we will be. This belief is what drives our degrees, reading, night school classes, weekend seminars, and such. Knowledge is the key to self-fulfillment.

Right at the start, we run into our first problem: what kind of education is it that will lead us to the greatest self-fulfillment? There are many things that we could study: auto mechanics, cosmetology, zoology, mathematics, psychology, economics. Without God, who, for the Christian, is the knowledge pathway to human flourishing, we are left to ourselves to sort out what is the best education that will lead us to the fullness of life. We will soon agree that the process of choosing the best line of knowledge is subjective and could change throughout our lives. Besides, each field of study will clamor that it is what we have been seeking, and if we miss it as our choice of learning, we will miss out. The choice of choosing an educational pathway is overwhelming.

Furthermore, we come to the problem that all pathways have, which is the answer to the question of self-fulfillment. What is it, and how do we know we have it? Should we know what self-fulfillment looks like? How do we know that it will last?

Educational pursuits toward fulfillment are meant to be objective, but we experience them subjectively. No two people who have studied chance theory will experience the same quality of satisfaction. One person will be more fulfilled than the other.

Lostness is not only something that Jan and I experienced on those mysterious paths through the Palatine Forest years ago; it is who a person is at the center of his life experiences. With Pride as Your guide, we come to the stark realization that we have been duped. Pride has not only led us astray to the point of lostness, but it has also subtly deceived us. We have become pawns of his in the game of life and have lost. Our deception is called auto-regeneration: the self sustaining itself by itself (*self*-fulfillment). We have come to the end of our journey, and it has ended where it began: with us.

G.K. Chesterton related the story of the yachtsman who set sail from the English coast, intending to sail to an exotic South Seas island. After many days, he sighted land, quickly beached his boat, and headed inland. Before him stood a dreaded pagan temple. He scaled its walls and bravely planted the Union Jack at its pinnacle. Only then did he realize that what he had scaled was the Brighton Pavilion on England's south coast! He thought he had sailed in a straight line, but because of an unfortunate miscalculation, he had actually traveled in a circle.[16]

Pride leads us, in search of ourselves, to end up where we started: with ourselves.

Jason Lehman clothed the longing and the dilemma of pride in his poem, "Present Tense."

It was spring, but it was summer I wanted,
The warm days, and the great outdoors.
It was summer, but it was fall I wanted,
The colorful leaves, and the cool, dry air.
It was fall, but it was winter I wanted,
The beautiful snow, and the joy of the holiday season.
It was winter, but it was spring I wanted,
The warmth and the blossoming of nature.
I was a child, but it was adulthood I wanted,
The freedom and the respect.
I was 20, but it was 30 I wanted,
To be mature, and sophisticated.
I was middle-aged, but it was 20 I wanted,
The youth and the free spirit.
I was retired, but it was middle age I wanted,

The presence of mind without limitations.
My life was over, but I never got what I wanted.[17]

Going Deeper

Questions are *quests* toward deeper insight and better application. Individually or as a group, the following questions invite you to wade into greater depth of understanding.

- Describe a time in your life when you were lost. Recall the emotions you had. What did being lost feel like?
- What is it like for you to be on a journey toward self-fulfillment?
- Of the five paths toward self-fulfillment illustrated in this chapter, which one have you preferably traveled and why?
- What did it cost you to take the path you were on toward greater self-fulfillment?
- Reread the poem "Present Tense" at the end of this chapter. Can you relate to the longings described in the poem? Give examples.
- What one aspect of lostness has become important to you? At your next convenience, discuss this aspect of lostness with a close friend.
- Have you gotten out of life that which you wanted? Explain.

Chapter 3

Darkness

"And now hundreds of cries rose at once. The death rattle of an entire convoy with the end approaching. All boundaries had been crossed. Nobody had any strength left. And the night seemed endless."
ELIE WIESEL[1]

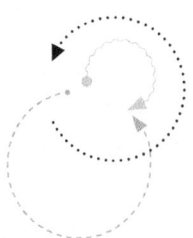

I recently met Harper. Harper is twelve years old, yet she admits to being "almost thirteen." Harper lives with her family on the lake, where our family has had a cottage for almost fifty years. She is also currently going through confirmation classes, learning the Ten Commandments and the Apostles' Creed by heart. I asked Harper if I could ask her a question. "Sure" was her response. So, I dove in: "If you could ask God one question, what would it be?" Long silence. Then she replied, "I would ask God, how will the world end?" What a great question!

With Pride as our guide, we now come to entertain Harper's question slightly reformulated: how will the world of the proud, the overconfident end? Answer: it will end with the greatest climate change imaginable. It will end not just in darkness but in outer darkness. All will be intolerable, abject night.

Eliezer was fifteen years old when he, his mother and father, along with his little sister, Tzipora, were herded into boxcars on a train in their

47

native Hungary. They were on their way to unbelievable horror—places that could only be aligned with hell—places like Birkenau, Auschwitz, and Buchenwald. His family was annihilated, their remains ascending the crematoriums of Nazi concentration camps. Elie survived, but his belief in God did not.

On April 11, 1945, American soldiers entered the concentration camp of Buchenwald near Weimar, Germany, and freed Elie along with other remaining Jewish captives. Elie vowed to remain silent for thirteen years, internally attempting to process and ultimately give voice to unspeakable horror. Then he spoke. In 1958, he published a slim volume called *Night*.

We listen in stunned silence to his words:

Never shall I forget that night, the first night in camp, that turned my life into one long night seven times sealed.

Never shall I forget that smoke.

Never shall I forget the small faces of the children whose bodies I saw transformed into smoke under a silent sky.

Never shall I forget those flames that consumed my faith forever.

Never shall I forget the nocturnal silence that deprived me for all eternity of the desire to live.

Never shall I forget those moments that murdered my God and my soul and turned my dreams to ashes.

Never shall I forget those things, even were I condemned to live as long as God Himself.

Never.[2]

The only thing worse than the death of millions of Jews in the hands of their Nazi tormenters is the fate of those people who have put themselves at the center of their lives—the proud, arrogant, self-righteous, overconfident people of this world.

Only twice in the Gospels do we read of Jesus being astonished. The Son of God, who knew all things, was moved to amazement over His hometown people's refusal to believe in Him despite His miracles (Mark 6:6). In contrast to the Jews in Capernaum, Jesus was *astonished* at the faith of a Roman centurion, a non-Jew, who, though he had not seen Jesus, placed his faith in Jesus. As a result, the soldier's servant was healed. Jesus said of this man, "I have not found anyone in Israel with such great faith" (Matthew 8:10). Contrastingly to those in Israel who were Jews but refused to believe in Jesus, "the subjects of the kingdom will be thrown outside, into the darkness, where there will be weeping and gnashing of teeth" (Matthew 8:12). The subjects can only be meant ironically. These are religious people who considered themselves to be subjects of God's kingdom, but in reality were not.

For those who are full of themselves and empty of honoring Jesus (our definition of a proud person), the journey ends with darkness. But it is a new quality of darkness—outer darkness, as in utter darkness. Jesus said of Himself that He was the light of the world and His followers would "never walk in darkness" (John 8:12). Darkness is that place reserved for those judged by God to be unfit to live in His presence because they have rejected His grace. These are the people who have, during their life on earth, said they will have no part in Jesus, and Jesus, the Judge, retorts that He is extending their wish into eternity. He will have no part of them in His kingdom. "Outer darkness was one of the expressions Jesus used for hell, since it is an absolute exclusion from the light of God's presence."[3]

In Jewish cultic life, we learn of various concentric circles of those who made up the worshipers at the temple in Jerusalem. The holy of holies was that place in which the high priest was allowed entrance into the very presence of the Lord in the form of the tabernacle. He was allowed entrance once a year. The next circle was the court of men, followed by the court of women. At the fringe on the outer section was the court of the Gentiles, where God-fearing non-Jews were allowed to worship. The least access to the presence of God was reserved for those in the outer court.

Darkness is the absence of light and, as such, is the epitome of disorientation. Once, as a teenager, I was in the wilderness of northern Wisconsin on a moonless night. Along with others, we ventured into the woods with our flashlights. At one point, our guide told us to extinguish our sources of light. There we stood in complete darkness. In one word, it was *terrifying*. We had no way of knowing where we were or how to proceed from where we were.

If we could visualize a place of absolute darkness, we would sense the horror of being alone without direction. The "weeping and gnashing of teeth" of which Jesus spoke concerning those who were judged and sent to outer darkness speaks of the deep and abiding regret of those who have reached their final destination—to themselves, deprived of God. It is also a description of remorse, which is derived from two Latin roots: *re-* for "again" and *mordere,* meaning "to bite." It means one's conscience is "biting one" again for actions done in the past. The pain of pride is doubly woeful—regretting that which one did to end up in a place of such abject darkness and then being pained by an unrelenting consciousness that reaps unending self-accusation.

The great Oxford don, C. S. Lewis, wrote,

If the universe is not governed by an absolute goodness, then all our efforts are in the long run hopeless. But if it is, then we are making ourselves enemies to that goodness every day, and are not in the least likely to do any better tomorrow, and so our case is hopeless again. We cannot do without it, and we cannot do with it. God is the only comfort; He is also the supreme terror: the thing we most need and the thing we most want to hide from. He is our only possible ally, and we have made ourselves

His enemies. Some people talk as if meeting the gaze of absolute goodness would be fun. They need to think again. They are still only playing with religion. Goodness is either the great safety or the great danger—according to the way you react to it. And we have reacted the wrong way.[4]

Darkness is an apt description of a person who is separated from God. Such darkness has its genesis in this present life. We consider the words of Jesus, where He spoke of Himself in the third person:

Whoever believes in him [i.e., Jesus] is not condemned, but whoever does not believe stands condemned already because they have not believed in the name of God's one and only Son. This is the verdict: Light has come into the world, but people loved darkness instead of light because their deeds were evil. (John 3:18-19)

Jesus was absolutely clear on this: before a person ends up in eternal darkness, he, in this life, does things that show his love for darkness (evil deeds).

Jesus saw Himself as the judge of all humanity. His favorite way of describing Himself in the Gospels is "the Son of man." What did He mean by this? This self-definition has a reference point in the prophetic book of Daniel. Daniel, a Jewish exile in Babylon, was overcome with a vision from God. In this vision, he saw what we understand to be kingdoms that will rule the earth (Babylon, Medo-Persia, Greece, and Rome). At the apex of these kingdoms is a king who rises and speaks boastfully (pridefully). We pick up the narrative in Daniel chapter 7.

Then I continued to watch because of the boastful words the horn [i.e., the king, ruler] was speaking. . . . In my vision at night I looked, and there before me was one like a son of man, coming with the clouds of heaven. He approached the Ancient of Days and was led into his presence. He was given authority, glory and sovereign power; all nations and peoples of every language worshiped him. His dominion is an everlasting dominion that will not pass away, and his kingdom is one that will never be destroyed. (Daniel 7:11, 13-14)

When Jesus referred to Himself in the Gospels as "the Son of man," He was drawing on this portion of Scripture in Daniel 7, the Son of man as judge of all the earth. As a judge, Jesus is both a lawgiver and a law enforcer. Before Jesus as judge, at that name which is above every name, every knee will bow in heaven and on earth and under the earth (Philippians 2:9-10). For some, this will be the event to top all events in their lives—Christmas, Easter, birthdays, raises, and weddings combined. For others who have lived for themselves, it will be abject humiliation.

The Bible makes it abundantly clear in both the Old and the New Testaments that God will not abide pride. "The LORD detests all the proud of heart. Be sure of this: They will not go unpunished" (Proverbs 16:5). King Nebuchadnezzar of Babylon, the most powerful man of his time, was humbled by God after he had demanded his subjects worship him as a deity. God struck him down, and he became insane for seven years, eating grass like a beast (Daniel 4). At the end of his humiliation, God restored the king's sanity. Nebuchadnezzar learned the hard way that pride goes before a fall, and he said, "Now I, Nebuchadnezzar, praise and exalt and glorify the King of heaven, because everything he does is right and all his ways are just. And those who walk in pride he is able to humble" (Daniel 4:37).

Commenting on Jesus, who has been assigned the task of judging all people by the Father, James Packer stated, "When the Bible pictures God judging, it emphasizes his omniscience and wisdom as the searcher of hearts and the finder of facts. Nothing can escape him; we may fool men, but we cannot fool God. He knows us and judges us as we really are."[5]

The Apostle Peter wrote during a time of immense persecution of the church through the caesars of Rome, who set themselves up as gods. Christians refused to worship the emperors and were thus hounded and often put to death. Quoting a passage in the book of Proverbs, Peter wrote, "God opposes the proud but gives grace to the humble" (1 Peter 5:5, ESV).

But why is the sin of pride so pernicious in God's eyes, demanding those full of themselves to be separated from God eternally? Cornelius Plantinga gave us cogent reasoning for this.

All sin has first and finally a Godward force. Let us say that *a* sin is any act—any thought, desire, emotion, word, or deed—or its particular absence, that displeases God and deserves blame. Let us add that the disposition to commit sins also displeases God and deserves blame, and let us therefore use the word *sin* to refer to such instances of both act and disposition. Sin is a culpable and personal affront to a personal God.[6]

Let us dwell on this for a moment. We were given a beautiful gift, handmade as it were by God, which we call life. In this life, we have experienced a treasure trove of good things and people that have saturated our lives with abundance. Beyond such great gifts, we have been wooed into a loving relationship with the Father God, who has created and sustained us up to this present time. All throughout our lives, He has been reaching out to us to call us back to Himself as the fulfillment of every dream we have ever dreamed, the satisfaction of every longing we have ever had, and the joy of all our desires. And we have said, "No, thank you. I'll live my life on my own terms, figuring out what is best for me. And what is best for me is to live this life without you. Goodbye, God."

Among many character qualities of Jesus, we know Him to be a gentleman. When a person says to Him, "Leave me alone, I'd like to live my life on my terms without Your help or presence," Jesus, with heart breaking, acquiesces. He grants them their wish.

The prideful person sits on his own throne. He edifies himself.[7] The essence of pride is seen in the determined occupation of the throne, which rightfully belongs to God alone. Not only has he dethroned God, but the person of pride is now at war with God—resisting Him at every turn. As the *Übermensch* (Nietzsche), he is fighting to be in charge and to stay in charge of his life. Career choices, relationships with others, finances, passions, goals, and what makes life good are poured into the funnel of self. The full-of-himself self has no room for another God. He has beaten the competition. He is the captain of his destiny. But what he discovers too late in life is that his destiny is darkness.

Cause	Effect
God is great	Light Orientation Joy
I am great	Darkness Disorientation Remorse

Figure 7. Cause-Effect

Revering either God or ourselves puts us on a trajectory that will end with us reaping what we have sown. The above diagram illustrates this truth. The humble person will essentially put God above all things and thus live in submission to Him. The proud person, in contrast, will put herself above all things and only have herself as her north star. The logical conclusion of where a life lived with self at its center will take us is not where anyone intended to go. The proud person is fully convinced that she can have all the benefits of a Godward life but without God. She has bet the farm that her life will end in light, orientation (clarity), and joy. How great the disappointment and pain when, in the end, the harvest is not plentiful but pitiful. "Though the pride of the godless person reaches to the heavens and his head touches the clouds, he will perish forever, like his own dung" (Job 20:6-7). Sober words.

How Does One End Up in Outer Darkness?

Separation from God for all eternity is not something that just happens, like clicking off a switch and, in a second, the room becomes dark. Pride is the gradual macular degeneration of the soul that ultimately leads to blindness toward God and darkness from God. What are some of the blind spots that a proud person does not perceive?

Loss of Perspective

People with pride suffer from myopic vision; they have become nearsighted. For nearsighted people, what is far away appears blurry or fuzzy; for the proud, this is the case as well—God and the reality that emanates from Him are not in focus. Instead of looking through a telescope to gaze upon a world of wonder and awe that takes them beyond themselves, they would rather use a microscope and look at themselves closely. The eros self is inordinately fixated on self-fulfillment.

Insecure, navel-gazing people make much of themselves. Douglas MacArthur, the commander of American forces in the Pacific during World War II, is a legend in the minds of most U.S. citizens. MacArthur was both an extraordinarily brave and resourceful leader as well as someone who had an overextended view of himself. He used fifteen-foot mirrors to heighten his image and "increasingly spoke of himself in the third person ("MacArthur will be leaving for Fort Meyer now"). . . . His belief in an Episcopal, merciful God was genuine, yet he seemed to worship only at the altar of himself. He never went to church, but he read the Bible every day and regarded himself as one of the world's two greatest defenders of Christendom. (The other was the pope.)"[8]

What is small under the microscope becomes bigger than life in the heart of a proud person. Blurred vision translates into reality skewed. Jay Gatsby was convinced that if he had enough money and was able to shine excessive wealth into the path of those in his orbit, he could conquer the heart of Daisy. He turned out to be rich in wealth but poor in outlook. All was manipulation masquerading as opulence turned inward. The core of his life was self-love. And it crushed him (as it will crush us).

Loss of Grace and Perception of Sin

"According to traditional Christian wisdom, a main problem with pride is that it recognizes neither sin nor grace; in fact, pride hammers them flat and discards them."[9] Sin is not falling short of the glory of God and being in need of salvation, but rather either an embarrassment or an affront to self-esteem. It gets in the way and thus must be taken away and discarded like yesterday's trash.

The same goes for grace. Pride leaves no room for grace, which is unmerited love and favor from God. For pride to entertain grace as an option would mean that there is a deficiency in who I am. Pride, however, is self-salvation, which excludes the need for someone like Jesus, who is God, to die for my sin to save me unto Himself. If there is salvation, pride will tell us that it is manageable.

Loss of Independence

Pride hates constraints. The place of eternal separation from God, which we refer to as hell, is a place of freedom. Lewis wrote, "I willingly believe that the damned are, in one sense, successful, rebels to the end; that the doors of Hell are locked on the *inside*. . . . They enjoy forever the horrible freedom they have demanded, and are therefore self-enslaved just as the blessed, forever submitting to obedience, become through all eternity more and more free."[10]

The freedom of which Lewis spoke is the freedom *from* God, which God grants. Yet Jesus taught us His model prayer that God is our Father, meaning we are His dependents: "Our Father in heaven . . ." (Matthew 6:9). For the Christian, there is no independence but only dependency on the One who makes us and saves us.

Pride chafes at any sort of dependency. It wants life on its terms, like the hamburger chain touts, "Have it your way." There is no other way but that which pride maps out and adheres to, which leads to self-satisfaction.

Loss of Worship

Pride is an equal opportunity lender. What it lends is worship—bowing down and obeying what is considered to have ultimate worth and supremacy. The Jewish nation had a unique calling. It was created and formed by God to live in worship of God as its supreme glory and good. The misery of Israel is that its people rejected the Lord and began to follow the idols of the nations around them. The Old Testament prophet Isaiah railed against the sin of pride in the life of Israel.

Israel had attached itself to what it had produced—money, superstitions, power, and supremacy.

> Their land is full of idols; they bow down to the work of their
> hands, to what their fingers have made. So people will be brought
> low and everyone humbled—do not forgive them. (Isaiah 2:8-9)

In Jesus' day, many of the religious elite worshiped wealth. The foil they had produced to deflect from their idolatry was religiosity. Luke said of the Pharisees that they loved money and sneered at Jesus and His teachings (Luke 16:14). Jesus responded by saying, "You are the ones who justify yourselves in the eyes of others, but God knows your hearts. What people value highly is detestable in God's sight" (Luke 16:15).

Then Jesus illustrated the debauchery of the religious leaders by telling them a parable. It is the parable of a rich man and a poor beggar by the name of Lazarus. The description of the rich man fits the lifestyle of the Pharisees: "dressed in purple and fine linen and lived in luxury every day" (Luke 16:19). Both die. The rich man ends up in hell (or hades, the place of those forsaken by God—the place of outer darkness). Lazarus was found at the side of Abraham, the father of the nation of Israel. We do not know the name of the rich man. His identity is known by his idolatry—"the rich man," now without riches. The poor beggar, however, has a name: Lazarus, meaning "God has helped." Hell is the place in the universe that is filled with people who are descriptions of what they loved, devoid of their proper names. Heaven is the place in the universe where people are known as individuals and have worth because they value the One who is supreme, the Lord Almighty, the maker of heaven and earth.

French artist Auguste Rodin ranks among the world's most gifted sculptors. He lived at the close of the nineteenth century. Many of us are familiar with his bronze figure of a naked man, slightly bent over, with one elbow resting on his knee and his chin cradled on his closed fist. The statue that we refer to as *The Thinker* is twenty feet tall and took thirty-seven years to complete. *The Thinker* is perched above a giant door. The door is the centerpiece of a complex multitude of figures below. He is contemplating the fate of those who are separated from God for all eternity.

The place of isolation from God in the next life is what Jesus referred to as hell. Peter Kreeft, a much-respected theologian and philosopher from Boston College, wrote, "Of all the doctrines in Christianity, hell is probably the most difficult to defend, the most burdensome to believe, and the first to be abandoned."[11] We all struggle with the doctrine of hell. Despite how difficult the notion of hell is, we cannot abandon it.

Jesus spoke much about the reality of hell. After describing the final judgment in Matthew 25:31-46, Jesus said that the unrighteous "will go away to eternal punishment, but the righteous to eternal life." Jesus clearly taught that every person will be held accountable for his or her earthly life and that every person will spend eternity in one of two destinations: heaven or hell.

The parable of the wedding feast in Matthew 22:11-13 teaches us three things about hell. First, hell means exclusion. Second, hell is darkness. Third, hell involves anguish. Heaven, or the consummation of the kingdom of God, is described in this parable as a kingly banquet feast. The king has provided a sumptuous feast, enough for many guests to celebrate his son's wedding. Servants are sent out to tell the invited guests that right now is the appointed time to attend the celebration. But they make excuses and refuse to come. Angrily, the king sends his servants out to invite another set of guests, the good and the bad, probably referring to Jews and Gentiles. Finally, the banquet hall is full of celebrants, all dressed in the proper wedding attire.

Then the king comes upon a man who is in attendance but is not dressed in the required wedding garment. He has no explanation as to why he would slight the king and his son in this way. The king has the man thrown out: "Then the king told the attendants, 'Tie him hand and foot, and throw him outside, into the darkness, where there will be weeping and gnashing of teeth.' For many are invited, but few are chosen" (Matthew 22:13-14).

If heaven is metaphorically described as a wedding banquet, complete with joyous feasting, then the expulsion from such a feast is hell. It is a place of darkness, which suggests both panic and disorientation. And lastly, it is a place of anguish—"weeping and gnashing of teeth"—sounds of utter remorse.

With Pride as our guide, we have come to the end of his tour. The glossy advertisements—those that touted the land of pride as frisky, fun, adventurous, and fulfilling—have woefully deceived us. Pride is no bedazzling diamond; rather, it is a tawdry zircon—a cheap imitation of the real thing. We have realized that our guide, Pride, has exploited us and duped us into believing we were on the verge of paradise when it was a garbage dump to which we were led.

The real thing is what the rest of this book is about: humility. Where better to start exploring this new and beautiful land than by looking at its shining light—Jesus?

Going Deeper

Questions are *quests* toward deeper insight and better application. Individually or as a group, the following questions invite you to wade into greater depth of understanding.

- Suppose you died and found yourself at the reception desk of heaven. The person behind the desk says to you, "Why should I let you into God's heaven?" What is your response?
- If your response has to do with anything that is performance-based—"my goodness, my generosity, my being better than others, my church-going," etc.—you will not get in. Imagine for a moment what it would mean to be judged by God to be insufficient because you have lived your whole life self-sufficiently. You are sentenced to utter darkness. What emotions are welling up inside of you?
- Utter darkness has been described as loss. Which of the four losses is most distressing to you and why?
- The good news is that you are not currently living in utter darkness, separated from God. There is still time to change the trajectory of your life. But how are you going about it?
- If this chapter ultimately leads to despair, what is hope for you?

Section Two: Learning to Go Low

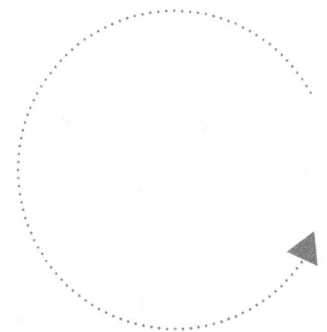

The book of Hebrews in the Bible is the book of superlatives. For it is here that Jesus is compared with angels, with Moses, with the Jewish high priest, and with the covenant between God and His people in the Old Testament. In each instance, Jesus is described as superior to these wonderous comparisons.

Is it any wonder then that the writer of the book of Hebrews challenged us to "consider him" (Hebrews 12:3)? We have just come from a wearisome journey and are exhausted. With Pride as our guide, we have considered what the enemy territory of humility consists of. It is an arid land, pockmarked by craters gouged out of the landscape by our own pernicious doing. We were promised the moon but ended up in hell. The land of pride was everything we never really wanted, and now we long for another land. It is our craving for a land of milk and honey, for the fulfilment of our wildest dreams, satiated with things the way they are supposed to be. Our longing is for a person. That person is Jesus, and Jesus is our teacher in what we sorely need: humility.

The dean of devotional literature, Andrew Murray, who wrote a seminal book on humility, encouraged us to look to Jesus and His humility.

Until Christians study the humility of Jesus as the very essence of His redemption, as the very blessedness of the life of the Son of God, as the only true relation to the Father, and therefore as that which Jesus must give us if we are to have any part with Him, that the terrible lack of actual, heavenly, manifest humility will become a burden and a sorrow, and our ordinary religion must be set aside to secure this.[1]

Now Jesus will be our guide. He will take us to four summits, from which we will survey the beauty of going low as evidenced in His life. From Jesus, we learn how to let go, to give over, to bend down, and to hold on.

Jesus has invited us to be His disciples. Disciples are students, learners, and, in true Jewish tradition, those who live with the master, learning from Him, but more than that, learning Him. The test of learning translates into behavior. Good students become like their teachers. As we follow Jesus, our master, He will take us into this new land. It is the land of His life, the land of humility, and this land is the joy of our desire.

Chapter 4

Letting Go

"Do you wish to rise? Begin by descending. You plan a tower that will pierce the clouds? Lay first the foundation of humility."
SAINT AUGUSTINE[1]

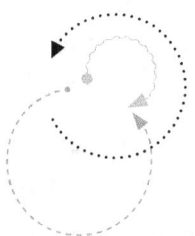

People everywhere looked up to him. At five feet and four inches, Louis looked over the heads of everybody around him. Those of taller stature than he bent over, which effectively made the man above others. King Louis the XIV was the most powerful, most feared, and most glorious person in seventeenth-century Europe. Most places he went, King Louis the XIV was carried. His feet literally hardly ever touched the ground. Servants dressed and undressed him, with hundreds of invited guests looking on. Those seeking his audience, when granted, had to walk backward toward the monarch, thus avoiding direct eye contact. His residence was an opulent palace outside of Paris, in Versailles. The reign of Louis the XIV was "the Grand Century," unrivaled in power, wealth, and prestige.

Before Louis was born in 1638, his mother had been barren for twenty-three years. His parents acclaimed him as "God-given." At the age of five, Louis became king while his mother remained co-regent. His mother educated him with the help of his godfather, Cardinal Mazarin. Louis liked to refer to himself as the "Sun King," for just as the planets revolve around the sun, so too did all people and things revolve around him.

Louis was the center of the universe. Reminiscing on the renown of his king, Primi Visconti wrote, "Both within and without the realm all were submissive to him. He only had to desire something to have it. Everything, down to the weather, favoured him. . . . Besides this, he had money, glory, and, above all, fine health; in short, he lacked nothing but immortality."[2] Louis knew himself to be God's ruler on earth and His representative. Loyalty to the Catholic Church moved him to violently, in the name of God, persecute Protestants. Louis the XIV's reign lasted until 1715, when, after seventy-two years on the throne, he died.

Contrast Louis the XIV with another king, much greater than Louis, the Son of Man, whose express mission was not "to be served, but to serve" (Mark 10:45). Whereas for a limited time in a specific place, people bowed low when in the presence of King Louis, all people who have ever lived will one day, conjointly with all other created beings, bow their knees in worship of King Jesus the Christ (Philippians 2:10).

Bathing in the glow of his majesty, the Sun King had droves of servants bending their knees in homage and service to him. The Son of Man, however, wrapped Himself in the apron of a domestic servant and, kneeling, washed the grimy feet of twelve of His followers (John 13). He, who could have called legions of angels to rescue Him from the fangs of murderous men, voluntarily stretched out His arms on an instrument of death to allow spikes to be driven into His wrists. He who made the heavens and the earth and the black hole that is thirty billion times bigger than our sun gave us His calling card that has "I am gentle and humble in heart" printed on it (Matthew 11:29). Then He said, "Learn from me"— de facto, learn from the King of Kings what it means to be humble.

We desperately need to learn from Jesus what a good life is—a life that pleases God, a life of humility.

While in prison, the Apostle Paul penned one of the earliest hymns of the Christian Church. It is a hymn about Jesus in which Jesus is sung as the Lord of Glory who surrenders His glory to condescend to become a man to save those lost in sin before returning to His glory. The song is intended to illustrate Paul's admonition to the church in Philippi to live a life of humility: "Do nothing out of selfish ambition or vain conceit. Rather, in humility value others above yourselves . . . have the same mindset as Christ Jesus" (Philippians 2:3, 5).

On the heels of this introduction, we read of the attitude of Christ Jesus in His action: "Who, being in very nature of God, did not consider equality with God something to be used to his own advantage [something to be grasped]; rather, he made himself nothing by taking the very nature of a servant" (Philippians 2:6-7).

The phrase that interests us is found in the New American Standard Bible: "something to be grasped" or held on to. Jesus, being God while retaining His divine essence, did not cling to His status of divinity. He let go.

Let us, for a moment, think the unthinkable. Let us imagine King Louis divesting himself of his crown, his powdered wig, his throne, and his royal robes of sovereignty fringed with gold and precious jewels, and clothing himself with a loincloth to clean the latrines of the palace. It would be incredulous to imagine King Louis stooping to such abject denigration. Should we magnify Louis' glory and stature by one billion times, we would gain only a small glimpse of what Jesus Christ, the Son of God, had and let go of. Such a loss of dignity can only be deemed staggering, unfathomable, and utterly inconceivable. And yet Jesus did it.

It is in the human spirit to want to ascend. Only in the divine spirit do we perceive the glory of descent. In His humility, Jesus was contrarian to all that we view as successful. To get to us, Jesus had to become like us, and to become like us, He voluntarily and gladly shed Himself of all majesty, glory, honor, and dignity.

For God to make Himself into man is to humble Himself. The Greek verb *tapeinoo* (*"humbled himself"*) means "low-lying, that which is even or level to the ground." This term is used to describe the Nile River in ancient documents when it ran low.[3] Jesus' lowest point was when He became "obedient to death—even death on a cross!" (Philippians 2:8).

Contrast Jesus in His downward movement with that of the Greek pantheon. Zeus, at the apex of the pantheon, is immovable. Those gods closest to him remain in his vicinity. The lower segmented gods are those who are sent to earth to help manage the affairs of humans. Why? Because being with humans was punishment for lesser gods. Christianity flips the Greek worldview. The Lord of Lords, Yahweh Himself, not only came down to earth to visit but actually became a man to live among men.

Television's longest-running game show is *The Price Is Right*. The popular show, with over 9,000 episodes, premiered on September 4, 1972, with Bob Barker as the initial host. The idea behind the show is that contestants from a live audience are invited onto a stage that is decked out in merchandise. Very simply, those who guess the true price of products or are closest to that price, without going over, win the contest and garner cash and other prizes.

Perhaps we can imagine a conversation between the members of the Godhead. It could have been the Father who asked the Son and the Holy Spirit to consider what it would cost them to save a lost humanity. They all agreed that the only way to redeem humans stuck in the quagmire of their own doing was to send one of themselves to die in the place of the guilty. God sent Himself in the person of Jesus to pay the price.

In the game show, contestants' names are called by the host with the joyful imperative, "Come on down!" Now, why did the Father who sent the Son say to Him, "Come on down"? The reason is that the price was right. Salvation is the substitutionary atonement by our sinless and majestic Lord Jesus Christ to eradicate (pay for) the guilt we had heaped upon us before God by our sin. Sin means we were over our heads with debt so great that we could never, in a million years, repay it. The worth we have in the eyes of God the Father and the Son is seen in the quality of the sacrifice (payment) enacted by King Jesus to redeem us. Redemption is essentially an economic term, meaning something bought at a commensurate price. Our value to God is seen in the price that the Son of God paid to adopt us as His children. The price Jesus paid was the price of divestment that ultimately led to His death—He let go of His glory and majesty.

By letting go, Jesus was able to execute the greatest transaction in human history. His glory was turned into dishonor so that our dishonor might be exchanged for glory. To be loved with such magnitude teaches us to bask in the strength and beauty of knowing that we are worth the whole of the person of Jesus Christ. For the Father gave the Son for us (on behalf of us). "He offered himself as a sacrifice for us [gave Himself for us] a pleasing aroma to God" (Ephesians 5:2, NLT). Why did He descend? *For us*—for our benefit, because we could no longer be our own beneficiaries of debt canceled.

Let us ponder the ramifications of God letting go to lay hold of us. Two weeks after graduation from college, I married the woman of my dreams. Jan and I enjoyed courtship for almost four years before we were wedded at the relatively young age of twenty-two. We worked long and hard on writing our own vows. This is what I promised her that warm Saturday in June long ago:

Jan, God has chosen you to be His own before the foundation of the world, and now for these brief years of life, He has entrusted you to me. With His love evidenced in Christ as my model, I pledge to you that I shall relinquish my desires, my pleasures, and my possessions for your best interest as long as I shall live. I offer my life to you and endeavor to use it to nourish and cherish you. You may rest assured that my commitment to you will transcend any malady that life might bring, whether sickness, accident, or any other misfortune. With Christ being our Guide into all the holiness of life, I promise to faithfully lead you toward unity with Him and toward greater unity between ourselves. I love you, Jan, and I commit myself to walk in utmost faithfulness to you only as long as God gives me breath.

Now, after more than forty-three years of stumbling forward in my commitment to Jan, of the 153 words that make up my vow to her, it is the word *relinquish* that means the most. For me to relinquish my desires, pleasures, and possessions for Jan's best interest has been the most challenging feat in my marriage. I have often not gotten it right, wanting to retain rather than relinquish.

When Jesus let go, He relinquished a place of His own: heaven, saturated with unfathomable beauty. He left a community of undying adoration and love for Him, and He moved from the side of His Father to side with those who would knock Him down and throw Him out. When Jesus relinquished those things, He did not do it with teeth clenched. Rather, He did it with great joy. "Who for the joy that was set before him endured the cross, despising the shame" (Hebrews 12:2, ESV).

It's not so much what Jesus let go of but for whom He let them go that fueled His joy. We know that He did it out of a deep desire to please His Father in heaven. His Father was pleased with such commitment, for we hear His voice at the baptism of the Son saying, "This is My beloved Son, in whom I am well-pleased and delighted!" (Matthew 3:17, AMP).

Submission is another word describing Jesus in His relinquishing His world for our world. *Submission* is Latin for "a lowering, a letting down, sinking to the will of another." In marriage, it means heaven on earth. On earth, it means realized hope—the joy of Jesus will be our joy!

Further plumbing the depths of Jesus' descent, we discover an extension of His letting go. "He made Himself nothing" is parallel to "not holding onto equality with God." In a world where everyone wants to be someone, Jesus made Himself nothing.

I remember the day I made myself nothing. Jan and I and our three young children had moved to the city of Mannheim, Germany, in the early 1990s to start a new church there. Always eager to contact new people, I found a great way to go about having significant conversations with Germans who were disenfranchised from Christianity. Dressed in a worn T-shirt and an old pair of jeans, I sat down in the pedestrian zone of the downtown area of Mannheim. Before me, I placed a basket with change in it. In front of me was a sign that read, "Have been greatly blessed; please help yourself."

I felt like I was mistaken for what was a normal occurrence in German cities: beggar. Vivid is the memory of about twenty people gathered around me having a conversation. Suddenly, an irate older woman broke through. Standing in front of me full of fury, with an umbrella raised menacingly, she railed, "How dare you sit there and beg? When I was your age, I worked for a living." A young man standing next to her turned to her and said, "But he's not begging; he's giving away money." The look on the face of that poor old lady was priceless. She was absolutely, utterly confused.

Looking up at those around me, I was able to explain myself. I told them that God had been good to me, and out of a heart full of gratitude, I wanted to display thanks by being generous. It was a great way to share the good news of the gospel, and the money I gave away was well worth the experience.

But that feeling of being looked upon as a poor person was painful. I felt a tinge of shame about what people thought of me. Jesus, having all the riches of heaven at His beck and call, had "no place to lay his head" (Matthew 8:20), and when He died, He only had the clothes on His back—and even those were confiscated. The price Jesus paid to go low was obscurity, going unnoticed, rejection, and being shamed.

FULCRUM OF GRACE

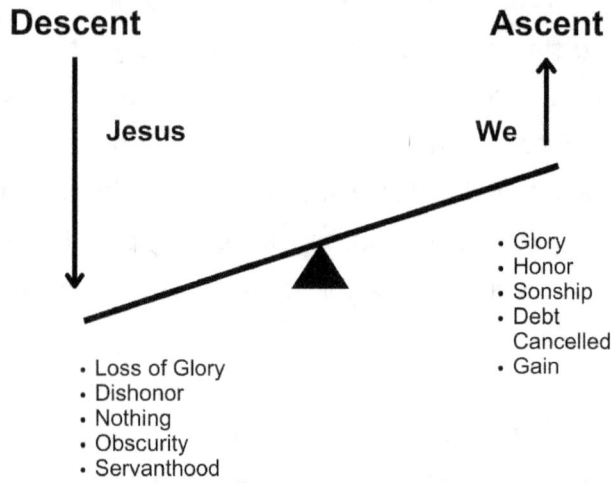

Figure 8. Fulcrum of Grace

The above diagram, which I refer to as the Fulcrum of Grace, looks like a teeter-totter. The middle of the teeter-totter is the fulcrum point, the place at the center of balance where, when one side has more weight, it elevates the other side. The greater weight is the weight of glory in Jesus' descent, in His letting go of His glory, His honor, His reputation, His status, and His stature. By exerting the greater weight, we are lifted and elevated to glory, honor, sonship, forgiveness, and eternal gain. Had Jesus not gone low, we would not be able to swing high.

But there is another element in the descent of the King of Kings that we need to consider. It is that Jesus took on the very nature of a servant. Jesus became poor so that we might become rich (2 Corinthians 8:9). Here we notice the loss of dignity and glory.

He was born in degrading conditions and placed in a feeding trough after birth. In terms of His appearance, Jesus would have never made it onto the cover of *Vogue*, *EQ*, or *Men's Health*. Seven hundred years before

His entrance into our world, the prophet Isaiah summarized, "He had no beauty or majesty to attract us to him, nothing in his appearance that we should desire him" (Isaiah 53:2). He had no property. Wealthy women supported Him and His disciples. And when He died, He died the death of horror and shame, naked to those watching Him expire on an instrument of torture in the brutal Middle Eastern heat. The last words He heard were words of maligning and taunting by the religious establishment of Jerusalem, by commoners, and by the soldiers executing their bloody job. "The people stood watching, and the rulers even sneered at him. They said, 'He saved others; let him save himself if he God's Messiah, the Chosen One'" (Luke 23:35).

How did King Jesus respond to such taunting? With silence. "He was oppressed and afflicted, yet he did not open his mouth; he was led like a lamb to the slaughter, and as a sheep before its shearers is silent, so he did not open his mouth" (Isaiah 53:7). After Pontius Pilate, who was appointed by the emperor Tiberius to be governor over Judea, interrogated Jesus, he sent Him to Herod, who was governor over Galilee. "He [Herod] plied him with many questions, but Jesus gave him no answer" (Luke 23:9).

The restraint shown by Jesus demonstrates His authority. He, who was in the right, did not need to set straight those unrightly wronging him. Rather, Jesus let go of His words and remained silent before His accusers.

I well remember hearing of a similar incident in the life of Dallas Willard. I was privileged to spend two weeks in a monastery in the vicinity of Los Angeles, along with twenty-five other doctoral students, with the legendary Dallas Willard. Willard was a world-class professor who, for decades, taught philosophy at USC. One day, a friend of Willard's was a guest in one of his classes. The class was nearing the end when one of his students opposed Dr. Willard openly. Dallas remained silent. Afterward, the friend who had witnessed the brash, inopportune malignment attack of the student asked Dallas why he did not put the young man in his place. Dallas Willard answered, "I'm practicing the discipline of not having to have the last word."[4]

The One who spoke the first word, the One who birthed the universe, was silent. Jesus let go of His dignity, glory, status, and the use of His words to justify Himself.

The world of seventeenth-century French aristocracy, in which all orbited around the Sun King, is not much different from our world today. Then, as now, people strove to gain and retain. Voluntary loss—relinquishing wealth, honor, and stature to expend themselves for the good of others—is as rare as sighting a white stag or, more embarrassing, having six toes on one's left foot.

Attaining and relinquishing each comes with a price tag. For those in Louis' court who wanted to better their lot in life, life was dangerous. Rarely do we consider the fear and danger of being among the privileged 1 percent. In Versailles, people contended with the fear of food poisoning, espionage, getting on the wrong side of the court's favor, shaming, and serial adulteries. The better life, the upward life, was costly all the way around. But so was the life of Jesus, who let go. It cost Him everything. But for those of us who, in great awe and wonder, have entrusted ourselves to His care, it has meant immeasurable gain. Wasn't this what Jesus meant when He said, "If you cling to your life, you will lose it; but if you give up your life for me, you will find it" (Matthew 10:39, NLT)?

The real winners are those who have hitched their wagon to the One who, for their sake, let go. For therein is joy for evermore. It's like hitting the jackpot on a ticket that was purchased by another. Indeed, it was. His loss is our gain.

Going Deeper

Questions are *quests* toward deeper insight and better application. Individually or as a group the following questions invite you to wade into greater depth of understanding.

- In comparing the two kings, Louis the XIV and Jesus the Son of Man, what jumps out at you?
- What did Jesus relinquish in His search for you?
- When was the last time you "let go" of something that was rightfully yours so that someone else could benefit from your sacrifice?
- What in your estimation keeps you from letting go?
- Do you think you can make it a goal this week to practice the spiritual discipline of not getting in the last word? What would that look like?

Chapter 5

Giving Over

"May all of your expectations be frustrated,
May all of your plans be thwarted,
May all of your desires be withered into nothingness,
That you may experience the powerlessness and poverty of a child,
And can sing and dance in the love of God
The Father, Son and Holy Spirit. Amen."
BRENNAN MANNING[1]

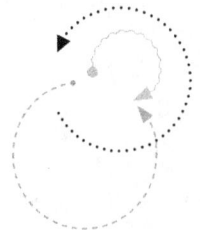

She lit up the room wherever she went. Muriel was vivacious, cheerful, energetic, and wise. People were drawn to her effervescent personality and spunkiness. Then things began to change. The program director at the local Christian radio station was one of the first to notice. While taping her weekly devotional, *Looking Up*, Muriel seemed befuddled. Either she repeated herself or there were uncomfortably long pauses in her presentation. Her husband, Robertson, got a call from the program director. A meeting between the two resulted in the program director telling Robertson that he thought it best to take the program off the air. When Robertson heard the reasoning behind his comments, things began to add up.

It began when, during a vacation in Florida with another couple, Muriel repeated a story that she had just told five minutes ago. It was Robertson's first alarm that something was not right. Medical professionals were consulted, and they came to the frightening conclusion that Muriel

75

was suffering from the onslaught of Alzheimer disease. At age fifty-five, Muriel's public ministry was over; no more conferences, TV, or radio.

In the ensuing months, the diagnosis was confirmed even as it was painfully being witnessed by those in the community of Columbia Bible College, where Robertson was the president. It got so debilitating that Muriel succumbed to panic attacks when Robertson was no longer near her. Despite the assistance of a caregiver, which allowed Robertson to continue his duties at the college, Muriel broke away and sought out her love. Then things became untenable. Muriel could no longer be constrained. She would walk from her home to see Robertson at his office on campus, sometimes five times a day. So great was her drive to be with him that she would break into board meetings just to be near him.

Robertson had to come to a decision. It was either the college or Muriel. He could no longer shoulder both. As he told it, it was an easy decision to make. He relinquished (there we have that word again) his position as president of a prestigious educational institution to become Muriel's full-time caregiver. His reasoning was communicated to the students in a chapel message he delivered:

> The decision was made, in a way, 42 years ago when I promised to care for Muriel "in sickness and in health . . . till death do us part." So, as I told the students and faculty, as a man of my word, integrity has something to do with it. But so does fairness. She has cared for me fully and sacrificially all these years; if I cared for her for the next 40 years I would not be out of her debt. Duty, however, can be grim and stoic. But this is more: I love Muriel. She is a delight to me.[2]

For the next twenty years, as Muriel continued to descend into the abyss of her crippling illness, Robertson lovingly cared for her. In the end, she could no longer speak or move but needed to be fed, washed, and diapered like a baby.

Robertson's deep love for Muriel is reflected in his book *A Promise Kept*, in which he wrote,

Twenty summers ago, Muriel and I began our journey into the twilight. It's midnight now, at least for her. Sometimes I wonder when dawn will break. Even the dread Alzheimer's disease isn't supposed to attack so early and torment so long.

Yet, in her silent world Muriel is so content, so lovable, I sometimes pray, "Please, Lord, could you let me keep her a little longer?" If Jesus took her home, how I would miss her gentle, sweet presence. Oh yes, there are times when I get irritated, but not often. It doesn't make sense. And besides, I love to care for her. She's my precious.[3]

The promise to love Muriel no matter what was the impetus for Robertson to quit his presidency in order to engage fully with his wife as her caregiver. By doing so out of love, Robertson engaged his will.

We do not always live up to our profession of faith, but we always live up to what we believe. Though it may sound confusing, it really is quite simple. Faith is seen in behavior. What we truly believe is reflected in observable activity. The will is the muscle of faith. Much like Jesus, Robertson's love was seen in his response to adversity: "Father, if you are willing, take this cup from me; yet not my will, but yours be done" (Luke 22:42).

In going low, in His heart, the will of the Father was conjoined with the will of the Son. This is why Jesus descended in the first place: "For I have come down from heaven not to do my will but to do the will of him who sent me" (John 6:38).

In the Old Testament, we find a collection of Scripture that we refer to as wisdom literature. These five wisdom books are Job, Psalms, Proverbs, Ecclesiastes, and Song of Songs. The New Testament extrapolates the theme of wisdom, enlarging it by making an astonishing statement: Jesus Christ is the personification of wisdom!

Paul wrote, "Christ the power of God and the wisdom of God" (1 Corinthians 1:24), and that in Him are "hidden all the treasures of wisdom and knowledge" (Colossians 2:3).

The theme of the book of Proverbs is "The fear of the LORD is the beginning of knowledge, but fools despise wisdom and instruction" (Proverbs 1:7). Wisdom means walking with God, being in awe of Him, and living in intimacy with Him. "Do not forsake wisdom, and she will protect you; love her, and she will watch over you. The beginning of wisdom is this: Get wisdom. Though it cost all you have, get understanding" (Proverbs 4:6-7). Commenting on this, Hebrew scholar Derek Kidner wrote, "What it takes is not brains or opportunity, but a decision. Do you want it? Come and get it."[4]

Jesus, living in awe and intimacy with His Father, made the decision: Your will be done!

Where we see this in action is on the path leading up to Jesus' crucifixion. He had just washed His disciples' feet and introduced them to the new covenant in the form of the Lord's Supper. Jesus is "the Lamb of God, who takes away the sin of the world," meaning their sin as well (John 1:29). Now, before He was to be taken captive by soldiers, we see Him cloistering Himself in conversation with His Father.

The scene in the Garden of Gethsemane is the consecration of the will. Jesus said, "Father, if you are willing, take this cup from me; yet not my will, but yours be done" (Luke 22:42). This is not a place of resignation or panic but of comfort and strengthening.

Yet it was a season of great inner turmoil for Jesus. We see Him praying with heavy anguish (or agony) that His "sweat was like drops of blood falling to the ground" (Luke 22:44). John Stott has us considering the forceful words that describe strong emotions with two comments. "The first, which Luke records, was that he had 'a baptism to undergo' and felt 'distressed' (or 'pressed', even tormented, *synecho*) until it was completed. The second was a saying which John records that his heart was 'troubled' (or 'agitated' *tarasso*), so that he even wondered if he should ask his Father to save him from 'this hour.'"[5]

In today's world, this is not the way that most people do it. They do not put their trust in an all-caring and all-knowing God but take things into their own hands. They seek solutions—ways in which to escape the pain. Or if resigned to it, they see it more as fate than providence.

Jesus was in deep sorrow, but He was not anxious. He was doing what the disciple who denied Jesus, Peter, wrote about: "Humble yourselves, therefore, under God's mighty hand, that he may lift you up in due time. Cast all your anxiety on him because he cares for you" (1 Peter 5:6-7). Jesus was refusing to take things into His own hands. Instead, He was confident that God's mighty hand would lift Him up in due time (which we later learn was three days).

When in a tight spot, we often panic and start to devise ways of escaping. This is the default mode of the wicked or the proud person. She can't just sit there; she needs to find a way out. Proverbs 28:1 says, "The wicked flee when no one pursues, but the righteous are as bold as a lion." In Gethsemane, Jesus, the Lamb of God, was bold as a lion. He was a righteous man. The (righteous) straightforward man, like the lion, has no need to look over his shoulder. What is at his heels is not his past but his rear guard: God's goodness and mercy.

The Psalms were the prayer book of Jesus. He knew that Psalm 23 ended with "Surely your goodness and love will follow me all the days of my life, and I will dwell in the house of the LORD forever." But "follow me" is too weak of an expression for the Hebrew wording here. The text literally means God's goodness and love will *pursue* me all the days of my life. Jesus rested in the quiet confidence that in every moment of His life, the Father was pursuing Him with goodness and love. That was His rear guard.

> The essence of the good news is that God the Son humbled Himself to the cross for us, and the essence of the good life is that we must humble ourselves in the service of others. In fact, we are told, that the very same humble mind that characterized Christ is now to characterize us. We are to renounce selfish ambition and conceit and, in humility, consider others better than ourselves (Philippians 2:3-11).[6]

Before straining for His last breath, Jesus devotedly said, "Father, into your hands I commit my spirit" (Luke 23:46). They were His last words.

Luke told us that Jesus "called out with a loud voice" (Luke 23:46). Before His last outburst, both creation and the temple—the place where Yahweh dwelt with His people—cried out with a loud voice. The sun stopped shining (too bashful to shine light when the Light of the World was shining in His darkest hour), and the curtain of the temple separating worshipers from the holy of holies was torn in two. Darkening and ripping—the sun and the temple were heralding the last words of their king.

We all are destined to speak our last words.

We contrast the way Jesus died with the defiance of Dylan Thomas in the face of his father's impending death. Anger and obstinacy were Dylan Thomas' weapons against death. Thomas was a brilliant Welsh poet who died at age thirty-seven of complications related to alcohol abuse. Although he quit school when he was only sixteen, his love of words propelled him into the realms of great literary acclaim both in Britain and in the United States. The impending death of his father was the context for the creation of one of the world's most famous poems (Do Not Go Gentle into That Good Night) surrounding death. Here is the first stanza.

Do not go gentle into that good night,
Old age should burn and rave at close of day;
Rage, rage against the dying of the light.[7]

The entire poem consists of six short stanzas. Thomas chose the word *rage* eight times to clothe his disdain toward death. Rage is understood as an expression of helplessness couched in defiance. Nonetheless, in the end, death will have its way, despite how Thomas or we rail against it. How do we cope with the inevitableness of death in a way that brings relief?[8]

The eight last words of Jesus while dying on the cross provide us with an alternative to rage—and it is trust. If, when we die, all we have left is ourselves, then rage and despair are the only appropriate responses. But if there is another with whom we have been intimately connected who described Himself as "the way and the truth and the life" (John 14:6), then His life is our life—life eternal.

The promise Jesus made to those who have placed their trust in Him is life with the Father. "No one comes to the Father except through me" (John 14:6). It is this Father that Jesus addresses in His last sentence: "Father, into your hands I commit my spirit" (Luke 23:46).

What do we learn about dying in the death of Jesus? We learn that dying is never a solo experience; it is accompanied by a loving Father who is our intimate companion.

There is a story told about a little boy who lay in the throes of death. His parents asked their pastor to come and be with their son and speak words of comfort to him before he died. The pastor came and went straight to the dying child's bedroom. Alone together, the pastor took the little boy's hand and recited the first five words of Psalm 23. As he did this, the pastor laid hold of each finger one by one. Gripping the boy's thumb, he said, "*The* Lord—there is just one God and no other gods beside Him." Then the boy's index finger, "The *Lord*—the one who is master of all that happens and master of your life." Laying hold of the middle finger, the pastor said, "The Lord *is*—now in this moment; He is here." Grasping the ring finger, he said, "The Lord is *my*—He is your very own personal friend and the God who loves you dearly. You are dear to Him." Lastly, he took the child's little finger, saying, "The Lord is my *Shepherd*—He watches out for you and concerns Himself with you. He will never leave you or abandon you. He will never do you evil, hurt you, or lose you. He is waiting to wrap you in His arms. After this, the pastor prayed with the boy and left him.

The next morning, the pastor received a call from the boy's parents, who informed him of the death of their son. After a long pause, the father of the boy asked the pastor if he could help them understand something. Early in the morning, when they went into their boy's bedroom, they discovered that the boy had died with his hand grasping the ring finger of his left hand. "Can you explain what this might mean?"[9]

In addressing God as *Father,* Jesus was "clutching His ring finger."

In giving over, Jesus consummated a lifetime of surrender to His Father by surrendering one last time. He was always, in every situation and circumstance, committing His spirit into the hands of the Father.

In the 1970s, the most popular song on the radio was Led Zeppelin's iconic "Stairway to Heaven." Robert Plant's lyrics—combined with his unsurpassed guitar solos of various genres, the shifting of all four gears on the register of intensity, and the mysterious meaning of the words— have embedded themselves in the soul of America.

> There's a lady who's sure all that glitters is gold
> And she's buying a stairway to heaven[10]

Try as we might, we strain to figure out what Robert Plant wanted to convey. We know that "sometimes words have two meanings."

What Plant does is awaken a metaphor for home (heaven) that is resident deep within the soul. But it is Jesus whose life and words, especially His last words, convey to us a sure stairway to heaven that He ascended and where He now waits for those who have given themselves over to Him in faith.

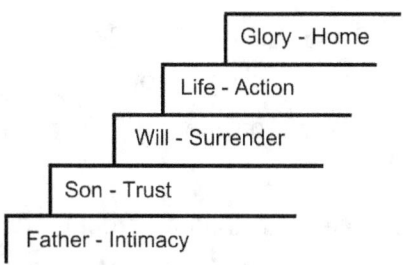

STAIRWAY TO HEAVEN

Figure 9. Stairway to Heaven

God's longing for intimacy with us translates into an invitation to us. C. S. Lewis illuminated:

Christ says, "Give me All. I don't want so much of your time and so much of your money and so much of your work: I want You. I have not come to torment your natural self, but to kill it. No half-measures are any good. I don't want to cut off a branch here and a branch there. I want to have the whole tree down. I don't want to drill the tooth, or crown it, or stop it, but to have it out. Hand over the whole natural self, all the desires which you think innocent as well as the ones you think wicked—the whole outfit. I will give you a new self instead. In fact, I will give you myself: my own will shall become yours."[11]

Here we have it. The great surprise in surrendering our will to God is that God gives us Himself! What could be greater than God? No 401(k), no honeymoon in Cancún, no winning the jackpot, no dream home will ever come close to the satisfaction of belonging to God as our Father because He gave us His best—Jesus.

Going Deeper

Questions are *quests* toward deeper insight and better application. Individually or as a group, the following questions invite you to wade into greater depth of understanding.

- Read aloud Brennan Manning's quote at the beginning of this chapter. What disturbs you about it? What delights you about it?

- Assuming that there is no willpower, but that the will responds to what the heart loves, as Robertson did for Muriel, how important was it for Jesus to will what the Father wanted Him to do? "I have come down from heaven not to do my will but to do the will of him who sent me" (John 6:38).

- When you look at Figure 9, "Stairway to Heaven," can you describe how the various steps are manifested in your life?

- What makes the quote by C. S. Lewis at the end of this chapter such a watershed in your life of intimacy with the Father?

- Do what the pastor did with the boy dying on his bed to the individual fingers of your hand. With your eyes shut, squeeze each finger as you emphasize the words "The Lord is my shepherd." What happens when you get to *my*?

Chapter 6

Bending Down

"What you tell me about in the nights. That is not love.
That is only passion and lust. When you love you wish to do things for.
Your wish to sacrifice for. You wish to serve."
ERNEST HEMINGWAY[1]

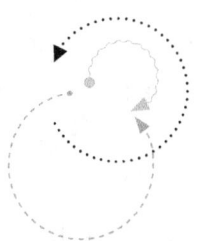

I doubt if I would have been born, save for Germany's defeat at the end of the Second World War by Allied forces. My parents, both born and raised in Germany, hailed from opposite ends of the country. My father was born in a small village in western Germany, in the Black Forest region, close to the French border. My mother, however, was born in Silesia, which is on the eastern fringe of the country.

In 1944–45, the Russian Red Army was making significant advances into German territory. The leaders in my mother's small village heard rumors that it would likely be a few weeks at most until the enemy had reached their village. Horror stories abounded about what enemy soldiers did to young girls. The leaders decided that the village would collectively flee to the Sudetenland in the Czech Republic until it was safe to return. They left on February 10, 1945, hoping that they would be gone just for three weeks until the danger had abated. Three hundred and fifty villagers, including my mother, who was thirteen at the time,

85

her older sister, their mother, and their father were among them. They never returned.

They lost everything. They lost their house, their land, and their thriving wholesale fruit and vegetable business. Perhaps most significantly, they lost their beloved *Schlesien*, their homeland.

My grandfather's truck was loaded down with their most precious possessions. They were on their way back to my grandfather's family in the Black Forest, where there would be food, shelter, and an extended family, when German troops confiscated the truck (needed if the Wehrmacht was to succeed). The four of them continued westward on foot, eating old potatoes and sleeping in barns, open fields, or, if fortunate, on the floors of hospitable strangers.

Malnourished, sick, weary to the bone, and exhausted from nine months of trekking, they were welcomed by family in the Black Forest. Here, they began a new life in what was for my mother, her sister, and my grandmother a new dialect, a new religious environment (they were Lutheran but surrounded by Roman Catholics), and new beginnings.

My grandparents found employment for their young teenage daughter in the small castle estate of the Baron and Baroness of Diersburg near Offenburg. Despite earning a small weekly wage that she gave to my grandparents, my mother was essentially an indentured servant, working for food and lodging. She served the Baroness, which meant dressing and undressing her, bathing her, and being at her beck and call. A bell would ring, and the Baroness would call out, "Fräulein Thea!" My mother would jump up from where she was and run to royalty calling. It was bone-weary work from early morning to sometimes midnight. She was also expected to clean, wash, serve meals, and watch over their firstborn son.

Servanthood took a toll on my mother. She remained sickly, plagued by an unyielding cough, looked pale, and lost even more weight. After a year of service, my grandmother mercifully put an end to her daughter's employment.

A couple of years later, my parents met on a dance floor, courted, were engaged, and married before immigrating to Milwaukee, Wisconsin, in 1955, journeying on the *Queen Elisabeth* to New York. I was born three years after they reached the promised land. I doubt if I would have been born had Germany not lost the war.

Servanthood took a toll on my mother. It will take a toll on us. It certainly took a toll on the Son of Man (the King—not a baron!) who "did not come to be served, but to serve, and to give his life as a ransom for many" (Mark 10:45).

When the Apostle Paul sent his business card to the church in Rome, otherwise known as the book of Romans, he was writing to people he had not yet met. But he was on his way there to stand trial before Caesar. In chapter 1 of Romans, Paul introduced himself by highlighting five things that defined him, the first of which was servanthood: "Paul, a servant of Christ Jesus, called to be an apostle and set apart for the gospel of God" (Romans 1:1). Our English word *servant* comes from the Greek word *doulos*. Most commentators tell us that about 75 percent of the church in Rome was made up of Gentile Christians who were slaves. They were not indentured servants (like my mother was) but slaves—without freedom, income, or independence. They belonged to their masters indefinitely. Ironically, the first thing that Paul, a Roman citizen and therefore a free man, said was that he was as they were, a *slave* of Christ Jesus.

Paul was in great company because *doulos* is the word that Jesus used to describe Himself when He offered us His business card. As we consider Jesus' example in going low, we must consider the King as a slave to His Father when He came to serve us.

Jesus knew He was the delight of His Father. "You are my Son, whom I love; with you I am well pleased," His dad announced (Mark 1:11). Conversely, Jesus loved His Father. "The world may learn that I love the Father and do exactly what my Father has commanded me" (John 14:31). Love is behind Jesus bending down and becoming a servant.

The Lord, speaking through the prophet Isaiah, wrote of Jesus the Messiah seven hundred years before His arrival by referring to Him as His servant. "Here is my servant, whom I uphold, my chosen one in whom I delight" (Isaiah 42:1).

In the Old Testament, we learn that wealthy Jews sometimes employed slaves to work fields and help in the household. After six years of service, it was incumbent upon the master to release his servant, with one exception. Sometimes the slave pleaded to stay with his master. "But if your servant says to you, 'I do not want to leave you,' because he loves you and your family and is well off with you, then take an awl and push it through his earlobe into the door, and he will become your servant for life. Do the same for your female servant" (Deuteronomy 15:16-17).

An awl is a sharply pointed metal shaft held by a wooden knob. It is used to make holes in leather to augment the easier sewing of pieces to one another. Here, the same awl is used to bore a hole in the earlobe of the slave who wanted to stay with his master. We might think of it as a plug in the lobes of some people today, easily recognizable as something out of the ordinary.

We can easily imagine Jesus would have done that—joyfully allowing the hand of the Father to drill a hole in His earlobe. Jesus wanted to stay submitted and surrendered to the Father and at His beck and call because He loved and delighted in Him.

Love will go to great lengths, even to the point of enslavement. The genesis of the modern-day mission is anchored in the Moravian Brethren fellowship in Herrnhut, Germany, under the spiritual direction of Count Nikolaus Ludwig von Zinzendorf. In the time of the counterrevolution to the Reformation in the early eighteenth century, Zinzendorf opened his estate to those fleeing persecution. A community of tightly knit men and women was formed. They were not survivalists by nature but were possessed by a burning heart to reach the lost around the world. To secure free passage on ships to the destination of foreign lands, they sold themselves into slavery. The love of Christ compelled them to such depths of devotion.[2]

The New Testament speaks of two kinds of slavery: before conversion, believers are enslaved (*douloo*) to the elements of this world (Galatians 4:3), but after conversion, they are called to serve (*douleuo*) one another in love. It is as we look to Jesus, who served out of love for His Father and mankind, that we begin to fathom the depths of His bondage.

Eight Ways in Which Jesus' Servanthood Becomes Our Model to Follow

Much of what New Testament writers referred to when referencing Jesus as a servant came from the book of Isaiah, specifically chapters 52 and 53. "Yet it was the LORD's will to crush him and cause him to suffer. . . . For he bore the sin of many, and made intercession for the transgressors" (Isaiah 53:10, 12). Paul in Galatians explained this passage for us. It was Christ "who gave himself for our sins to rescue us from the present evil age, according to the will of our God and Father" (Galatians 1:4). The preposition *for* (Greek *hyper*) carries the sense of "in the place of."

All In

Jesus did for us what we could never do for ourselves—He substituted His life for our lives of condemnation to free us from the bondage of sin. He made Himself a slave to free us from our slavery. It is important to note that He "gave Himself." He did not give money, time, or even labor; He gave Himself. He was wholly all in. Jesus' heart and soul were meshed in His deeds to benefit us.

Others Focused

The only benefit Jesus had from His service to us was knowing that we would benefit from it. That was enough. Also, as we have already seen, Jesus was all about living in the joy of the Father and giving Him joy in return.

The diagram below, which contrasts the human condition with the divine encounter, helps us get a grasp on the others-focused nature of Jesus' servanthood.

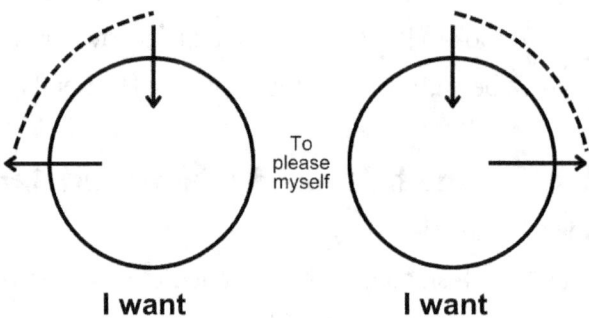

To please myself

I want   **I want**

HUMAN CONDITION

Figure 10. The Human Condition

In the human condition, it is the will to please myself that drives my volition. This can take the form of servanthood to the point that serving others garners a personal benefit that would otherwise not be realized. The suitor who presents his potential partner with a bouquet of roses at a substantial investment may use the flowers to win her over, hoping that she would then gratify him. Service can sometimes be utilitarian.

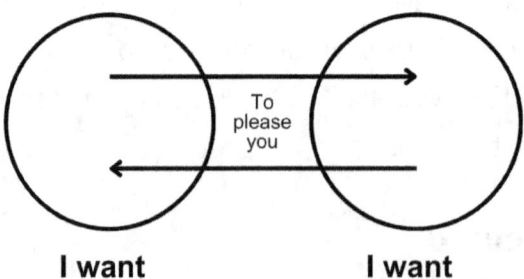

To please you

I want   **I want**

DIVINE ENCOUNTER

Figure 11. Divine Encounter

Contrast this with the divine encounter of servanthood. The second diagram shows us the Jesus way: I want to please the other. In desiring to please the other, Jesus let go of potential benefits. In fact, at the end of His life, His service got Him nailed to a cross, leading to great personal loss.

Christians should not be alarmed when service given reaps affront or even hostility.

Courage

The German word for humility is *demut*, which is derived from the old German *dienemut*, meaning "courage to serve." There was bravery in Jesus' servanthood. Every time Jesus set out to bless others, He opened Himself up to being misunderstood or even wounded. We remember that Jesus was betrayed by a kiss from a friend.

Depletion

Jesus experienced strength going out of Him in serving others. When the woman sick with a hemorrhaging blood disease touched His cloak in the midst of a crowd and was healed, Jesus responded, "Someone touched me; I know that power [to heal] has gone out from me" (Luke 8:46). After another prolonged time of healing people of their sicknesses and diseases, Jesus got into a boat and promptly fell asleep, exhausted by ministry. His batteries were so drained that even the storm and the gale-force winds that came up to toss the boat on the Sea of Galilee could not stir Him. His disciples had to physically shake Him awake, crying, "Lord, save us! We're going to drown!" (Matthew 8:25). And after having spent forty days in the desert fasting, "he was hungry" (Matthew 4:2).

Ministry is exhausting. It was for Jesus, and it will be for us.

One of the great gifts Jan and I, along with our three children, cherished was our three-week summer vacations in various parts of Europe. I remember one vacation after which I had preached evangelistically in a one thousand-person tent in Würzburg for ten days straight. I was totally spent. Right after that campaign, we drove our van down to Italy to get on a ferry that would take us to the island of Corsica for a three-week vacation. I will never forget sitting at the back of the ferry, watching the waves form and then disappear in the distance. Suddenly, I was seized by the thought that just sitting there and watching the wake go out felt illicit. I should be doing something. It was then that I realized how utterly exhausted I was, even to the point where I was misconceiving the gift of rest.

Always On Call

Jesus never clocked out. But He did not burn out either. When we look at Jesus during times when He was not serving, we discover His secret in serving: He refueled and refreshed His soul by seeking out His Father in solitude and by freeing Himself from the constraints of constantly having people around Him. The summary statement in the Gospel of Luke was indicative of Jesus' life: "Yet the news about him [Jesus] spread all the more, so that crowds of people came to hear him and to be healed of their sicknesses. But Jesus often withdrew to lonely places and prayed" (Luke 5:15-16). Vance Havner was fond of saying, "If you don't come apart . . . you will come apart!"[3]

Serving Is Loving

Jesus, as a servant, acted like a servant by serving. "Jesus knew that the hour had come for him to leave this world and go to the Father. Having loved his own who were in the world, he loved them to the end" (John 13:1). Then we see Jesus wrapping Himself with a towel around His waist to do what a household servant would have done when guests arrived after a dusty journey: He washed their grimy feet. His lesson to His disciples, even to Judas, who was plotting to betray Him, was abundantly clear: "Very truly I tell you, no servant is greater than his master, nor is a messenger greater than the one who sent him. Now that you know these things, you will be blessed if you do them" (John 13:16-17).

Love goes low. Jesus showed His love by doing the menial tasks of caring.

Serving Is Leading

Jesus empowered His disciples by serving them. Thus, He displayed a new paradigm of leadership: servant leadership.

> The defining mark of the Christlike character that Christian leaders are called to embody is self-sacrificial love. The suffering servant Jesus pointed His disciples to His own example as the paradigm for leadership. Instead of using political maneuvering and personal charisma to accomplish one's own agenda, the Christian leader seeks to advance God's purposes through self-sacrificially using all available resources. The result is a beautiful and compelling picture of Jesus the servant, who loved us and gave Himself for us.[4]

Service Is an Act of Worship

The altar is the place where a gift undefiled is given up unto the Lord in worship. Jesus was both an altar and gift unto His Father. In giving Himself up, He elevated the Father, glorifying Him. "When you have lifted up [crucified] the Son of Man then you will know that I am he and that I do nothing on my own but speak just what the Father has taught me. The one who sent me is with me; he has not left me alone, for I always do what pleases him" (John 8:28-29).

George Herbert was an Anglican priest who wrote beautiful poetry to the glory of God. In his poem "Love (III)," published in 1633, Herbert laid out a banquet scene. It is the heavenly feast written about the union between Christ and His Church. "Blessed are those who are invited to the wedding supper of the Lamb!" (Revelation 19:9). When describing this ultimate celebration, Jesus' story took an unexpected twist. The guest of honor, the Bridegroom, Jesus, the Messiah, is not served, but He is the servant serving His guests sumptuous platters of tasty delights. "It will be good for those servants whose master finds them watching when he comes. Truly I tell you, he will dress himself to serve, will have them recline at the table and will come and wait on them" (Luke 12:37).

By washing His disciples' feet on the eve of His crucifixion, Jesus illustrated the wedding supper of the Lamb by being His own server at His heavenly banquet.

George Herbert personified our heavenly Bridegroom as love.

Love bade me welcome. Yet my soul drew back
   Guilty of dust and sin.
   But quick-eyed Love, observing me grow slack
   From my first entrance in,
   Drew nearer to me, sweetly questioning,
   If I lacked any thing.

A guest, I answered, worthy to be here:
   Love said, You shall be he.
   I the unkind, ungrateful? Ah my dear,
   I cannot look on thee.

Love took my hand, and smiling did reply,
   Who made the eyes but I?

Truth Lord, but I have marred them: let my shame
   Go where it doth deserve.
   And know you not, says Love, who bore the blame?
   My *dear, then I will serve.*
   You must sit down, says Love, and taste my meat:
   So I did sit and eat. (emphasis mine)[5]

Recognized Herbert scholar Jim Orrick said of the last lines, "Love, who is, of course, the Lord Jesus Himself, reminds the reluctant guest that he bore the guest's shame on the cross, therefore the guest no longer bears it. The guest insists on assuming a low position at the feast—one of service. Love gently—but authoritatively—insists that the guest sit down and eat."[6]

Going Deeper

Questions are *quests* toward deeper insight and better application. Individually or as a group, the following questions invite you to wade into greater depth of understanding.

- Look at Figure 10, "The Human Condition." Can you relate an incident of late in which you wanted things to go your way?
- Revisit the descriptions of Jesus as a servant (slave). In what ways are you like Him as a servant? In what ways are you not like Him as a servant?
- Where are you exhausted? What do you need from those around you? From Jesus?
- What is so appealing to you about a leader who is foremost a servant?
- If service, rightly understood, is an act of worship, how well are you worshiping God?
- This week do something beneficial to someone close to you without getting caught and without talking about it. Pay attention to your motives and feelings.

Chapter 7

Holding On

"I said to Jan, 'I want to leave the ministry and go get a job at McDonald's. All I want to do is package hamburgers in cardboard boxes and not talk to anyone.'"
DIETRICH SCHINDLER

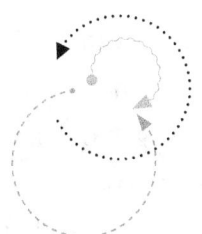

In the state of Washington, there sits the beautiful, awe-inspiring Mount Rainier. Mount Rainier is almost three miles high. It is the highest peak in the Cascade Range. Within the Cascades are twenty-five large glaciers, which make up the largest continuous ice field outside of Alaska. Whoever dares climb this colossal tower of ice must possess lots of alpine climbing experience and lots of courage. Donald Bennett is one of the men who has made it to the top of Mount Rainier.

But what is so extraordinary about his achievement is that he did it on only one leg! Donald Bennett is an amputee. On one stretch of the journey to the top, Donald and his team were confronted with a huge ice field that they needed to cross. To allow themselves the needed traction, each climber strapped metal cleats to the bottom of their hiking boots. Unfortunately for Donald, with two crutches and only one cleat strapped onto his boot, he was constantly slipping and falling. The only way for him to make progress was to fall forward on his face and pull himself up, thereby gaining three feet of progress. He did this over and over.

97

His teenage daughter, Kathy, was part of the climbing team. She saw the torture her father was going through and jumped into action. For the next four hours in which her dad fell forward and pulled himself up, Kathy was at his side, spurring him on, saying things like, "Dad, you're making it. You can do it. You're the best father in the whole world." Kathy's words touched Donald's heart deeply. In fact, it was her constant encouragement that enabled him to reach his goal.[1]

Encouragement is power. It is a power that overcomes our desire to give up. With encouragement, we can finish high school, grind through twelve-hour work-days, stay with people we love in difficult times, and achieve great feats like climbing mountains. Encouragement does so much for us, yet it's often hard to come by.

When things got beyond tough for Jesus, as He was on the path of pain and rejection and was about to undergo the extreme torture of crucifixion, the Kathy in His life, the one who was at His side, allowing Him to reach the summit for our salvation, was the Father.

> Let us run with perseverance the race marked out for us, fixing our eyes on Jesus, the pioneer and perfecter of faith. For the joy set before him he endured the cross, scorning its shame, and sat down at the right hand of the throne of God. Consider him who endured such opposition from sinners, so that you will not grow weary and lose heart. (Hebrews 12:1-3)

We fix our eyes on the goal—Jesus—in the same way He fixed His eyes on the Father. Reunion with the Father was the "joy set before him," which helped Him endure the cross.

The Uncomfortable Weight of Waiting

There are two words in the New Testament that are used when speaking of endurance or patience. One is *hupomone*, which means "to abide or remain composed under pressure." James used *hupomone* when he wrote, "Consider it pure joy, my brothers and sisters, whenever you face trials of many kinds, because you know that the testing of your faith produces perseverance" (James 1:2-3). The other word for endurance or patience is the word *makrothumia*. *Makro* means "large or long." *Thumia* means "suffering." *Makrothumia* then means "being long-suffering." The opposite is someone who easily flies off the handle. *Hupomone* has to do with difficult circumstances. *Makrothumia* has to do with difficult people.

Jesus exhibited both *hupomone* (which is the word for endurance in our text) and *makrothumia*. He remained steadfast under duress, and He suffered under the pain inflicted on Him by people.

A man of God who deeply affected both my life as a follower of Jesus and my ministry was Stuart Briscoe. Stuart and Jill moved from England with their three young children in the early 1970s to shepherd a small church in southwestern Wisconsin by the name of Elmbrook Church. Largely based on Stuart's extraordinary preaching and leadership gifts, the church grew to become the best-attended church in the state of Wisconsin. Billy Graham once supposedly said that Stuart Briscoe was one of the ten best preachers in America. I wholly agree.

At the age of ninety-one, Stuart was weakened by cancer but strengthened by Christ. In an interview a few months before his death, Stuart was asked by the interviewer, "Stuart, how are you doing under the circumstances?" Stuart answered, "I don't live under my circumstances. I live in them."[2] So did Jesus.

Years ago, when Jan and I had just started a new church plant in Mannheim, Germany, I had what I have come to refer to as my McDonald's days. The fledgling congregation was vibrant and growing. Many students and young families found their way to us, and many found new life in Christ. As a family, we went on our regular summer vacation and were refreshed. When we returned home, we found, as usual, a big stack of mail waiting for us. One envelope was particularly thick. The return address told me who it was from: a young couple in our fellowship, which was a key to what God was doing. She was a gifted worship leader. He was a small group leader and disciple-maker.

I opened the letter and discovered six handwritten pages, front and back. The couple criticized me and my leadership of the church. At the end of the letter, they declared that they were leaving the church. If that was not bad enough, I soon discovered that they had photocopied the letter and sent it to everyone in our church. I was devastated.

I said to Jan, "I want to leave the ministry and go get a job at McDonald's. All I want to do is package hamburgers in cardboard boxes and not talk to anyone." This went on for three days—during my "McDonald's Days."

We've all had them, and we will all have them down the road.

Having endurance means putting up with situations and people that make us angry and acting with grace and compassion toward them. Patience is the ability to throttle our motor when we feel like stripping our gears.

It does not mean that we let people or circumstances run all over us and treat us like doormats. We are made in the image of God, with great worth. We have the right to be treated with respect and to confront people when they abuse and disrespect us. We should try to get out of our burdens, if we can. For all other situations in life where that is impossible, there is patience.

Why is it so uncomfortable for us to bear up under the weight of having to wait or having to endure?

Out of Control (Powerlessness)

What makes waiting so uncomfortable is the fact that we are out of control. People or things exhibit pressure on us, not we on them. Waiting means that we must give in to a certain powerlessness of circumstances even as we wait on the Lord.

McDonalds Days

Figure 12. McDonald's Days

How are we bearing up? How are our hearts as we find ourselves in the waiting room? Waiting is weighty because we are out of control and powerless to change people or circumstances.

Out on a Limb (Uncertainty)

When we must wait, we are out of control and out on a limb. The problem with waiting is that it hardly ever comes with a schedule. But wouldn't that be nice? "Here's your timetable for the house hunt. You will notice that you will need to talk to fifty realtors, place five personal ads in the journal, spend hours driving around neighbourhoods, and after seven months of looking, you'll get what you want."

But it doesn't work that way. We never know when or if the waiting will end. We're out on a limb, given over to uncertainty.

Out of Our Minds (Anxiety)

And because we're out of control and out on a limb, we can be out of our minds with worry and anxiety. Waiting weighs on our minds. It can play games with our emotions. It can generate the juices of our fantasies. We begin to think of all the "what if" scenarios: What if there's no remission? What if the loan doesn't go through? What if the counseling won't help us? What if we don't get the adoption? Time spent in the waiting room can increase our anxiety levels significantly.

The Incredible Value of Waiting

The Bible has much to say about waiting. It tells us that there is incredible value in patience. "A patient man shows good sense, but a quick-tempered man displays the height of folly" (Proverbs 14:29, NCB). "A hot-tempered person stirs up conflict, but the one who is patient calms a quarrel" (Proverbs 15:18).

Tonight, someone is going to be made very happy. The state lottery will make someone a multimillionaire. But suppose that tonight there are two winners. A guy wins the jackpot—$10 million. A young woman is the second winner. They both go to pick up their winnings. He gets his check. Instead of a check for millions of dollars, she receives an unlimited amount of endurance. He's overjoyed. She is absolutely disappointed.

He goes out and purchases all sorts of things that he's always wanted but never had the money to buy: a new house, a big boat, a new car, lake property, and membership in a golf club.

The young woman, meanwhile, starts exercising endurance. Now, fast-forward ten years ahead. The millionaire is complaining about his high taxes. He has finally registered that many of his new friends are only in it for his money. He and his wife are so caught up in their affluence that they've drifted apart. He feels increasingly lonely and bored. Incredibly, on clear summer nights, he looks up at the stars, wondering what life would have been like had it stayed like it was before he won the jackpot.

And the young woman? She's done things she'd never been able to do before. She stayed in college, got good grades and a degree, and found a good job. Her marriage has been on an upward curve since she stopped screaming and yelling and started listening to her husband. She discovered that she has a caring heart for the poor and disadvantaged. She's also persistently pursuing God and is amazed at the joy and peace that Jesus has brought into her life. Her home is often filled with lots of friends who drop by because they love to spend time with her and her family. On clear summer nights, she looks up at the stars, wondering what life would have been like had she not won endurance.

If the choice is between the jackpot or endurance, take endurance. Because there is an incredible value in waiting.

Waiting Is Persevering

There are many things in life that only go to those who stay the course. We call it persevering. How do we land a good job? How do we build a solid and loving marriage? How do we lose weight? How do we not lose heart in prayer? The answer to all these questions is: perseverance— doing the difficult things in order to get to the good things.

Waiting Is Trusting

Jesus called men and women to be His disciples, His learners. One of the amazing lessons that His learners learned about a life connected to Jesus is that the Christian life is a two-story life. Most people in this world live a one-story kind of life. By that I mean, what they see, feel, and sense is all there is to life. They live within the confines of the physical world. But when the disciples began to spend time with Jesus, they were in for a big surprise, one with life-changing ramifications.

Utterly exhausted from a taxing day of meeting the needs of thousands of people, Jesus had His disciples push away from the shore in a boat to go to the other side of the lake. While they're rowing, He falls asleep. He's still sleeping when a huge storm gale descends upon them. The wind is howling. The waves are crashing into the boat. The boat is sinking. The disciples are screaming. Jesus is sleeping. So, they wake Him. Jesus raises Himself from His cushion and addresses the wind and the waves as if they were persons. In Mark 4:39, He commands, "Quiet! Be still!" In an instant, the wind stops howling, and the lake is a sea of glass. The learners are no more terrified of Jesus than they were of the storm. But what did they learn? They learned that there are two realities, two stories in which they live: the physical and the supra-physical. Many people do not realize that our physical world is encased within a much grander unseen spiritual world. Jesus then asked His learners this question: "Do you still have no faith?" (Mark 4:40).

Faith is trust. And trust means that I can entrust myself and my circumstances to the God of both stories. He is in control of all things. Hey, if He can speak to nature and calm it, then He is in control of both realms. Endurance says: "Lord, I trust You to be in control of my life and circumstances. Nothing can happen to me that has not first passed over the top of Your desk."

I can see things around me—painful, difficult things. I can hear. I can feel. But only Jesus knows what's really going on. I often don't. That's why trust is so important to those who wait. They believe that they are living in two stories, on two levels—and that Jesus is in control of both of them.

Waiting Is Progressing

When nothing is happening, that doesn't mean that nothing is happening. Waiting is progressing. We're always making progress when we wait. Often, God is at work when we're waiting. James chapter 1 tells us that we only mature as we patiently wait upon God to work things out that we ourselves can't work out.

Waiting Is Relaxing

Peace is concomitant to patience. What do you do when things are pressing in on you that you can't do anything about? You relax! Why? Because you can say, "Lord, You have promised to care for me and to care for my cares. I have cares. Now I'm in total anticipation of how You will show Yourself all-sufficient for all of my needs." Sometimes God saves us from this situation. And sometimes He saves us in the situation. But He'll always come through. So, relax.

The Supernatural Art of Waiting

But how do we learn to endure and to wait on God when people and circumstances make us angry and uncomfortable? Patience is a supernatural virtue that is brought about through the work of the Holy Spirit. The supernatural art of waiting is made up of three important aspects: sanctification, mentoring, and capitulation.

Sanctification—The Goal of Waiting

When we endure hardship, we put Jesus on display. "Fixing our eyes on Jesus, the pioneer and perfecter of faith. For the joy set before him he endured on the cross, scorning its shame, and sat down at the right hand of the throne of God. Consider him who endured such opposition from sinners, so that you will not grow weary and lose heart" (Hebrews 12:2-3). Waiting on God in difficult situations changes us as we wait. We become more like the One we wait upon. The lesson is this: if you want to make progress in being patient, don't center on patience. Center on Jesus. Because in centering in on Jesus, endurance comes softly into our lives in increasing measure.

Mentoring by the Holy Spirit—The Means of Waiting

Homer, in his *Iliad*, wrote about the warrior Ulysses, who goes off to fight in the Trojan War. Ulysses knows that going to war means leaving home for what will probably be years. His son is still young. Ulysses will not be around in his formative years. Thus, Ulysses appoints his servant, Mentor, to teach his son what it is to be a man of virtue.

The Holy Spirit is God's mentor sent to us to make us feel and behave like Jesus. As our mentor, He has a program of instruction that is unlike any educational curriculum we've ever experienced. We have often learned things serially and linearly, one step at a time. The Holy Spirit's mentoring seems random to us. He may bring a difficult person into our lives to gift us with the opportunity to learn compassion and patience. Think of a person who really irritates you. You'd give almost anything to get rid of him. But he's still around. Why? Because the Spirit of God means for him to be the gift of God to you. It makes sense. We can only learn to bear up cheerfully under difficult things and people when God allows us to have difficult things and people enter our lives. So, look for the difficult and uncomfortable mentoring opportunities brought on by the Holy Spirit to bring about patience in your life.

Capitulation—The (Small) Price of Waiting

There is a perseverance that is brought on by sheer tenacity and the power of the will. This is not the same as the patience wrought by the Spirit of God. Patience is not a product of human effort. It is the by-product of a person who is wholly given over to the Spirit of God. How is that done? By surrendering to Him—to His all-sufficiency, to His wisdom, to His presence.

Let us ask ourselves this question: "Where is God allowing us to live under pressure in order to produce endurance in us, and how can we cooperate with Him?"

Remember when we threw open the door of our lives to Jesus? We invited Him to come into our lives to transform us. Once Jesus was inside and had control, the doorbell rang. We opened the door only to find nine of His disciples wanting to come in as well. We soon realize that wherever Jesus is in our lives, these nine disciples hang out with Him. If Jesus has us and is alive in us, we will be visited by His friends, the nine disciples. We make room for them. We welcome them. The fruit of the Spirit comes in the form of the nine disciples: Love, Joy, Peace, Forbearance, Kindness, Goodness, Faithfulness, Gentleness, and Self-Control (Galatians 5:22-23).

We look to Jesus in the pain and pressure of living. He'll see to it that we have unlimited supplies of the power of endurance to cope.

Going Deeper

Questions are *quests* toward deeper insight and better application. Individually or as a group, the following questions invite you to wade into greater depth of understanding.

- Name some people who have cheered you on, who have been your encouragers.
- Have you ever had "McDonald's Days"? Explain.
- What are some things that greatly concern you but are out of your control?
- What are benefits to waiting patiently?
- Who in your circle of friends needs you to be their "Kathy," someone to come alongside and encourage them not to give up?
- What do you need to surrender that you cannot control into the powerful and loving hands of Jesus? Now, give that over Him.

Section Three
Learning to Go Low—
The Blessing of Descending

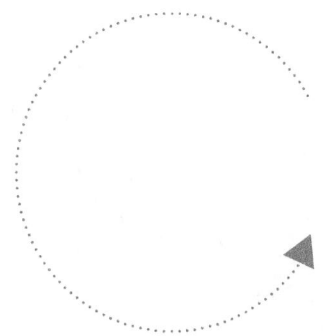

Now we enter the promised land. Here we hit pay dirt and find the gold we have been pursuing. Of the nine fruits of the Holy Spirit mentioned by Paul in Galatians, humility, although not explicitly listed, is the root of all the fruit.

In the first two sections of our journey, we have been asking and answering the questions of "What?" and "So what?" What is humility as opposed to pride? Humility is an accurate assessment of who we are in relation to God. We are low and lowly. The proud person assesses himself way too gratuitously, as the center of his universe, when, in fact, he is merely a speck of dust. We have uncovered the relevancy of humility in answering the question, "So what?" For those of us who follow Jesus, we follow a humble King who gave His life for us and who became nothing so that we would have everything of true value, supremely Him!

And now, in this last section, the rubber meets the road. This is where we answer the question, "Now what?" Wisdom, after all, is knowledge applied. In the Great Commission, Jesus didn't tell us to teach "everything I have commanded you"; instead He said, "Teaching them to obey everything I have commanded you" (Matthew 28:20, emphasis mine). If we have not applied what we have understood, we have not yet learned it.

Chapter 8

Humility Assessment

"'My life,' says Paul, 'is not controlled and determined by what is happening to me; I am in a state and condition in which I rise right above them. These things are not the determining factors in my life and experience.'"
D. Martyn Lloyd-Jones[1]

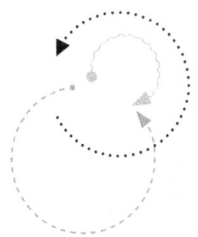

We have now come to the question of "Now what?"— where the rubber meets the road. For what good is it to know about the perniciousness of pride and to learn of humility in the life of Jesus if we do not see humility operative in our own lives?

Would people who know you well say, "Oh, she is a humble person; he is always thinking of others"?

If we were to cover ourselves with humility, we would do it much like we clothe ourselves with a suit or a dress. Before we buy either a suit or a dress, we are measured to make sure the size of the clothing will fit us. Why not do the same thing with the virtue of humility and thereby gain a proper appreciation of our stature so as to know how to address it?

Humility Self-Assessment

The following twenty questions will help us gain insight into where we stand regarding humility. Before we start, a few instructions are in order.

111

After each statement, there are three possible responses that run along a continuum from rarely (cold) to usually (hot). Do not think long and hard about what answer to choose; simply go with first impulses. When finished, it also may be helpful for someone close to us to fill out the assessment on us, thereby giving us a more objective view of ourselves. The key to analyzing our self-assessment is found at the end of this exercise.

It is important to answer the questions honestly without overthinking. Ready?

Questions

1. I do not get anxious when things get out of control.

        Rarely   Sometimes   Usually
          1   2   3

2. I like to help when I see someone in need.

        Rarely   Sometimes   Usually
          1   2   3

3. What others think of me does not define me.

        Rarely   Sometimes   Usually
          1   2   3

4. I avoid talking about my accomplishments.

        Rarely   Sometimes   Usually
          1   2   3

5. I do not get angry when something does not go my way.

        Rarely   Sometimes   Usually
          1   2   3

6. I live in regular communion with God.

        Rarely   Sometimes   Usually
          1   2   3

7. I am non-anxious when others leave me out.

Rarely	Sometimes	Usually
1	2	3

8. I pay attention to the motives behind my actions.

Rarely	Sometimes	Usually
1	2	3

9. I sense God's joy when I help others.

Rarely	Sometimes	Usually
1	2	3

10. I regularly praise God for who He is.

Rarely	Sometimes	Usually
1	2	3

11. I find myself deeply moved by beauty.

Rarely	Sometimes	Usually
1	2	3

12. I enjoy getting personally involved with people.

Rarely	Sometimes	Usually
1	2	3

13. Self-reflection is important to me.

Rarely	Sometimes	Usually
1	2	3

14. I rejoice when others succeed.

Rarely	Sometimes	Usually
1	2	3

15. I routinely experience joy.

Rarely	Sometimes	Usually
1	2	3

16. A sense of non-anxious well-being is pervasive in me.

Rarely	Sometimes	Usually
1	2	3

17. Though it stings initially, I welcome criticism.

Rarely	Sometimes	Usually
1	2	3

18. I ask God where I need to change.

Rarely	Sometimes	Usually
1	2	3

19. I enjoy giving (time, expertise, money, etc.).

Rarely	Sometimes	Usually
1	2	3

20. I think of God often throughout the day.

Rarely	Sometimes	Usually
1	2	3

Tallying Our Survey

Place the numerical value of our answers next to the question number in the five categories below.

Question Number   The Number We Gave Ourselves

Trembling

10

20

11

1

Helping

19

12

9

2

Discerning

18

13

8

3

Progressing

14

17

7

4

Celebrating

16

15

6

5

The highest total in any category would be a twelve and the lowest a four.

The operative word for a follower of Jesus is growth. Peter said as much when he wrote, "Grow in the grace and knowledge of our Lord and Savior Jesus Christ" (2 Peter 3:18). We are not seeking perfection, but we are against maintaining the status quo. We refuse to remain the person we have become. Thus, it is important for us who want to become more like Jesus in going low to first determine our most significant growth challenge. We discover our growth challenge by tallying up the results of the short survey we have just taken.

Which one of the five categories of behaviors is your weakest (the one with the lowest score) and needs attention?

Answer:_____

The following chapters can be read either serially or by beginning with our greatest need. The prize is advancement in humility, as it evidences the life of Jesus in us.

HUMILITY PYRAMID

Figure 13. Humility Pyramid

Chapter 9

Trembling

"As the sun angled, the buttes and coulees, the cliffs and sculptured hills and ravines lost their burned and dreadful look and glowed with yellow and rich browns and a hundred variations of red and silver gray, all picked out by streaks of coal black. It was so beautiful that I stopped near a thicket of dwarfed and wind-warped cedars and junipers, and once stopped I was caught, trapped in color and dazzled by the clarity of the light."
JOHN STEINBECK[1]

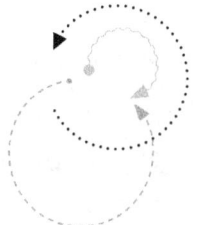

Our family was visiting the zoo in Heidelberg, Germany, one sunny Saturday morning. The two older children were grade-school age, and our youngest, Lukas, whom we were pushing in a stroller, was perhaps a year old. Zoos are where picture books come alive. Our children delighted in seeing the monkeys race, flinging themselves from tree to tree in hot pursuit of one another, a mother bird feeding its young in the nest, and penguins propelling themselves like torpedoes in the turquoise blue water. It was all beautiful, magical, serene, and peaceful.

We were approaching the lions' habitat when suddenly a male lion let loose a deafening roar. The deep turbine-engine-like shock waves were so forceful that they seemed to enter our bodies. Lukas was terrified and showed it by letting out his own piercing cry and then began sobbing. Indeed, we were all shaken. A ferocity of such magnitude, totally unexpected, frightened us. Though we tried to tell him that the strong iron fence kept the lion secure in his cage and unable to harm us, Lukas

117

was not having it. We had to take him up from his stroller and pull him close to us for him to begin to calm down.

What is more fearsome than a lion roaring?

God is.

I, the LORD, will roar like a lion. And when I roar, my people will return trembling from the west. (Hosea 11:10, NLT)

Blessed are those who have heard and felt God's roaring, those who are in awe of Him, people like Blaise Pascal.

Blaise Pascal was a seventeenth-century French mathematician who is credited with inventing the digital calculator (to help his father in his tax-collecting work), the syringe, the hydraulic press, and the roulette wheel. His contribution to the sciences was inestimable. Sadly, he died at the relatively young age of thirty-nine.[2]

After Pascal's death in 1662, his servant discovered a small handwritten note sewn into the lining of his favorite coat. What was on that piece of paper spoke of his conversion to Jesus Christ. It records Pascal's trembling and the awe of God that catapulted him into the arms of Christ.

Monday, 23 November, feast of St. Clement, pope and martyr, and others in the martyrology.

Vigil of St. Chrysogonus, martyr, and others.

From about half past ten at night until about half past midnight, FIRE.

GOD of Abraham, GOD of Isaac, GOD of Jacob

not of the philosophers and of the learned.

Certitude. Certitude. Feeling. Joy. Peace.

GOD of Jesus Christ.

My God and your God.

Your GOD will be my God.

Forgetfulness of the world and of everything, except GOD.

He is only found by the ways taught in the Gospel.

Grandeur of the human soul.

Righteous Father, the world has not known you, but I have known you.

Joy, joy, joy, tears of joy.

I have departed from him:

They have forsaken me, the fount of living water.

My God, will you leave me?

Let me not be separated from him forever.

This is eternal life, that they know you, the one true God, and the one that you sent, Jesus Christ.

Jesus Christ.

Jesus Christ.

I left him; I fled him, renounced, crucified.

Let me never be separated from him.

He is only kept securely by the ways taught in the Gospel:

Renunciation, total and sweet.

Complete submission to Jesus Christ and to my director.

Eternally in joy for a day's exercise on the earth.

Not forget your words. Amen.[3]

Learning humility has much in common with learning to be in awe of God and the fingerprints He has left behind on the majesty of creation—God's advertising agency.

The crisis of our age is that of boredom. So much of life is predictable and under our control. Thus, we vicariously seek excitement in sports, music, and sexual activity. In our digital, leisure-soaked, air-conditioned, therapeutic world, we have lost the gift of awe. Indeed, we have insulated ourselves from the terrifying, the wonderous, and the out-of-our-control forces of wind, storm, hail, and earthquake. They make us feel small and vulnerable. Vulnerability is not what we deem to be a good life, but it is for those who want to make advances in the virtue of humility.

Trembling awe is the basis for worship. The first disciples of Jesus experienced this firsthand. Having heard from some of the women who reported that the crucified and buried Jesus, whom they had been following, appeared to them in blazing glory, they were incredulous; that is, until Jesus made Himself known to them, uninsulated. "Then the eleven disciples left for Galilee, going to the mountain where Jesus had told them to go. When they saw him, they worshiped him—but some of them doubted!" (Matthew 28:16-17, NLT). The word *worshiped* means "to fall on one's knees or face in utter submission and surrender before a deity." It is reactive in its force; once God reveals Himself, we cannot help but throw ourselves on the ground in worship.

The playwright George Bernard Shaw referred to William Temple, the Bishop of Canterbury, as a "realized impossibility." Temple was renowned for his towering intellect, his ability to mediate between striking coal workers and their employers, and his spiritual leadership in the Church of England during the Second World War. Temple knew what real worship was.

Temple wrote,

Both for perplexity and for dulled conscience the remedy is the same; sincere and spiritual worship. For worship is the submission of all our nature to God. It is the quickening of conscience by His holiness; the nourishment of mind with His truth; the purifying of imagination by His beauty; the opening of the heart to His love; the surrender of will to His purpose—and all of this gathered up in adoration, the most selfless emotion of which our nature is capable and therefore the chief remedy for that self-centeredness which is our original sin and the source of all actual sin. Yes— worship in spirit and truth is the way to the solution of perplexity and to the liberation from sin.[4]

How do we wade into the waters of awe that lead to trembling and worship, making us small and God big? How can we be overcome by its waves, barely surviving, feeling Lilliputian and yet refreshed by the God who instills in us trembling awe of Himself?

Five Disciplines That Lead to Increased Trembling

Trembling awe is that which God gives to those who seek Him in His holiness. "If you look for me wholeheartedly, you will find me" (Jeremiah 29:13, NLT). God promises that He will let Himself be found, but under one condition—that we wholeheartedly (undividedly) look for Him. To look for God is another way of pursuing Him. The reward for pursuit is the treasure of finding God to be who He is—holy, awe-inspiring, and worthy of our worship.

The path of pursuit of finding God is made up of five disciplines, stoking us toward greater awe of God, taking us low: the Scriptures, meditation, imagination, posture, and prayer.

The Scriptures

The Bible is unique in quality among all literature. The Holy Scriptures are God's self-revelation, giving us insight into who He is and what He wants that is not generated by study. All other literature is the product of authors recording their thoughts, which is fine for that which exists on the horizontal plane of things. But when we come to the vertical, transcendent, otherworldly universe that is inhabited and filled up by God, reliable information can only come from the source of transcendence—God Himself.

When God speaks, people listen, tremble, and are in awe. "'Is not my word like fire,' declares the LORD, 'and like a hammer that breaks a rock in pieces?'" (Jeremiah 23:29). When God speaks, mountains quake, rivers overflow, fire breaks out, the earth opens its mouth to swallow sinners, and storms rise and are quelled. When God speaks, creation listens.

We will thus do well to take in the record of what God has said and done as preserved for us in the Bible, letting it wash up against our thoughts and impact our emotions.

How about calling out a year of trembling awe? In each month of the year, we would hone in on one awe-inspiring section of Scripture and camp out with it for thirty days. We would bathe ourselves in the awe passages morning and evening. In doing so, we would write down our observations, both in the texts we study and in our hearts, as they are impacted by God's Word. At the end of the year, we would collate our findings and produce a little book of awe that would serve us for the rest of our lives. God would be so much bigger, and we would be so much smaller as a result.

The following chart can function as our primer for awe inspiration for a year.

Month	Scripture
January	Genesis 28:10-19
February	Exodus 14:4, 19-31
March	Exodus 19:16-25
April	Deuteronomy 10:12-22
May	2 Samuel 7:18-29
June	2 Chronicles 7:1-3
July	Job 38
August	Psalm 8
September	Psalm 62
October	Psalm 139
November	Luke 7:1-10
December	Hebrews 12:22-29

Practical Application

Secure a notebook to record insights gleaned about God and your heart. In the first reading of the day, read the monthly passage of Scripture for insight. Jot down your thoughts in your notebook. In the second reading, toward the end of the day, jot down how the text is impacting your feelings and your heart.

Beginning with the Scriptures and what they tell us of our awesome God, the logical next step is to camp out and meditate on God's greatness and, in doing so, increase our access to awe.

Meditation

When we open the pages of the Bible, we read about the practice of meditation as if it were part of people's everyday lives. Isaac went out into the field in the evening and meditated (Genesis 24:63). The psalmist said, "I lie awake thinking of you, meditating on you through the night" (Psalm 63:6, NLT). And in another place: "I stay awake through the night, thinking about your promise" (Psalm 119:148, NLT). Jesus lasted forty days without food in the desert and resisted Satan with the statement: "Man shall not live on bread alone, but on every word that comes from the mouth of God" (Matthew 4:4). In plain language, man lives by meditating on God's Word. Peter went up on the roof of a house in the afternoon to reflect and pray (Acts 10:9).

Until our century, reflection on God, His Word, and His creation was an integral part of the spiritual lives of many. Hildegard von Bingen, Martin Luther, John Wesley, John Calvin, Madame Guyon, Brother Lawrence, George Fox, and Dietrich Bonhoeffer—all were people who made meditation a part of their lives. Meditation has always had great importance among Christians. It must gain new importance among us.

But all this time, I have been talking about meditation without describing what this term actually means. The term *meditation* is used variously in the Hebrew Bible. *Haga* is sometimes associated with the sounds of animals. Doves coo and lions roar (Isaiah 31:4; 59:11). However, it is also used for simply talking or speaking. But, in most places where this word is used, it has to do with concentrated thought.

This one word is variously translated: to hatch (Isaiah 59:13), to ponder (Psalm 142:5), to contemplate (Joshua 1:8), to think of (Psalm 63:7), to reflect back (Psalm 33:18), to lament (Jeremiah 48:31), to seek (Proverbs 24:2), to sigh (Isaiah 16:7), to grumble (Psalm 2:1), to ponder on (Psalm 38:13). Taken together, spiritual meditation is a concentrated reflection on God or His works, leading to inner strength and joy.

Meditation, therefore, has four components: excluding, listening, receiving, and being fulfilled.

We have all noticed that meditation is very popular as witnessed on talk shows, in popular stress-reducing books, and in the practices of Eastern religion. Meditation is enjoying a new upswing—but, unfortunately, not so much among Christians. Zen, yoga, and transcendental meditation have a very different conception of meditation than that of the Bible. In these forms, the goal is to get the brain and associated thoughts empty. In this state of nothingness, the meditator should detach himself from the burdens and pains of this world. He should let himself be absorbed into the impersonal cosmic, into the ground of all being. He has detached himself from his world and himself and has become one with the universe. Through this, man hopes for salvation from the suffering of this existence. This is Nirvana.

We notice the difference in what we call biblical meditation. Biblical meditation is not the dissolution of the self, but the inner gathering and alignment with a personal God. The Christian conception includes a mental liberation from oneself, whereas the Far Eastern religions do not have a connection to God. And it is precisely here, where the Christian engages with God, His Word, and His creation, that God gives abundantly. God instructs and empowers. He builds us up, not breaks us down. In finding Him, we find our true selves.

Contemporary man finds himself in the midst of this fast-paced society. Life is becoming more hectic, more restless, more crowded, and more distracted. As long as the devil finds us distracted, he basically does not need to do anything against us. The distraction is quite enough to keep us from having an intimate relationship with God.

Practical Application
I have found two very useful ways for me to lay down my worries and burdens. On the one hand, I have learned to write down a summary of the past twenty-four hours. By writing down my experiences and thoughts, I become calmer inside and more receptive. After that, I can usually think about God in a lighthearted way. Or another way: with my hands facing downward, I share my burdens with God. Then I point them upward and thank Him that He will give relief for every burden. This frees my heart.

These procedures open our hearts to an encounter with God. Here, it is important that we anchor our thoughts; otherwise, they will again float in the distance. There are some concrete ways to do this.

We bind ourselves mentally to God Himself. Psalm 63:6 says: "I lie awake thinking of you, meditating on you through the night" (NLT). We can take a characteristic of God and think about it. With concordance, we can choose passages that describe this quality.

We bind ourselves mentally to God's creation. Psalm 143:5 says: "I meditate on all your works and consider what your hands have done." The other day, I was sitting by a lake, blissfully alone. I closed my eyes and just listened to the soft murmur of the water against the shore for ten or fifteen minutes. Gradually, the sounds seemed to me as if they were a piece of joyful music. Afterward, I looked at the colored leaves as they fluttered down from the trees one by one, twisting and turning. They were also sights of joy. I was finally able to talk to my Master about it and rejoiced.

We bind ourselves mentally to God's Word. Psalm 1:2 says: "Whose delight is in the law of the LORD, and who meditates on his law day and night." We are convinced that the Bible is God's Word. It is His revelation to us, a love letter from His heart to ours. Therefore, we are richly endowed when we allow ourselves to be filled with the thoughts of God in the Bible. It is truth to us, where we sometimes lie to ourselves. It is comfort for us, where no one understands us anymore. It is strength for us, where we lack strength.

Imagination

Our world was created twice. The first creation was what God saw internally. The second creation was when He spoke, "And it was" (Genesis 1:31). As creatures created in the image of God, we too will learn to access our imagination to increase our awe of Him.

"To picture oneself" is the meaning of the Latin word *imaginari*, from which we derive our word *imagine*. To imagine something has to do with seeing with our inner eyes. The power of imagination lies in the fact that it transcends time and place.

Practical Application

Suppose we have studied Jacob alone in the desert, running from his vengeful brother, Esau. We have looked at the text in Genesis 28 where Jacob sees angels ascending and descending a ladder that reaches up to God in heaven. When Jacob awakens, he is shaken and says, "Surely the Lord is in this place, and I was not aware of it" (Genesis 28:16). Then we took the time to ponder this awe-inspiring incident in Jacob's life.

Now, with our imagination, we bring it home to our thoughts and emotions. Imagine we are Jacob. What is it that we feel after having a rock as our pillow? What do we smell at night? To what smells do we compare it? What do we hear, and how loud? What does the ground feel like? What are we looking at as we gaze above us?

As we imagine being in the place of Jacob, we mysteriously become him. His world is now ours to experience. Our hearts beat wildly as we feel God's very presence.

Posture

When people encountered God in His glory, they did not remain reclined in their easy chairs but responded verbally and bodily. When the prophet Isaiah saw the Lord high and lifted up, he blurted out, "'Woe to me!' I cried. 'I am ruined! For I am a man of unclean lips . . . and my eyes have seen the King, the LORD Almighty" (Isaiah 6:5).

The most common response to the holy presence of God was to fall down in terror and worship. The prophet Ezekiel did this on many occasions: "I looked and saw the glory of the LORD filling the temple of the LORD, and I fell *facedown*" (Ezekiel 44:4, emphasis mine).

As the angel of the Lord was punishing King David and all Israel for the sin of presumption in numbering the fighting men of Israel, David and those around him saw this angel's sword drawn. The chronicler wrote, "Then David and the elders, clothed in sackcloth, fell *facedown*" (1 Chronicles 21:16, emphasis mine).

The Lord in the Old Testament is Jesus Christ in the New Testament, so we conclude based not only on Jesus' own statements of Himself but on how people fell down before Him in worship. After a night's worth of fruitless toil, Peter was told by Jesus to put down his nets in the deep part of the Sea of Galilee. Reluctantly, Peter did this. The ensuing catch was of such magnitude that the nets began to tear and the two boats began sinking. "When Simon Peter saw this [catch of a lifetime], he *fell* at Jesus' knees and said, 'Go away from me, Lord; I am a sinful man!'" (Luke 5:8, emphasis mine).

When God is God and we are small, we respond boldly.

Practical Application

How can we learn to be in awe of God? One very easy and practical way is to literally go down on our knees or, better still, to fall prostrate on the floor in worship. We have already studied the Word of God, meditated on it, and imagined us being in it; now we appropriately fall down.

In lying prostrate before Him, we will confess, "Oh Lord, You are God. You are holy. You are glorious. I worship You!" As we hold out on the ground for five minutes or ten, the reality of who God is begins to overwhelm us. We feel Him, and as we feel Him, our awe of Him increases.

Prayer

In explaining the Ten Commandments in his *Small Catechism*, Martin Luther wrote poignantly of fear and love. Take the first commandment as an example. "You shall have no other gods. *What does this mean?* We should fear, love, and trust in God above all things."[5] In our trust in God, fear of Him is not antithetical to our worship of Him. To love and fear Him is to trust and obey Him. They go hand in hand.

What better way to learn to be in awe of God than by putting our thoughts into written prayer? If prayer is the language of the soul, writing our prayers will lead to greater passion and devotion.

Practical Application

On a regular basis, either daily or at most monthly, write out a prayer to God as worship of Him. We can use what Luther wrote to begin: "Oh Lord, I fear, love, and trust You above all things. Here are the reasons why . . ." After we have written down our prayer, we can then pray it out loud before Him as we worship Him in spirit and in truth.

We can summarize this chapter by envisioning its content as a tree, the tree of awe, and the disciplines suggested to climb it.

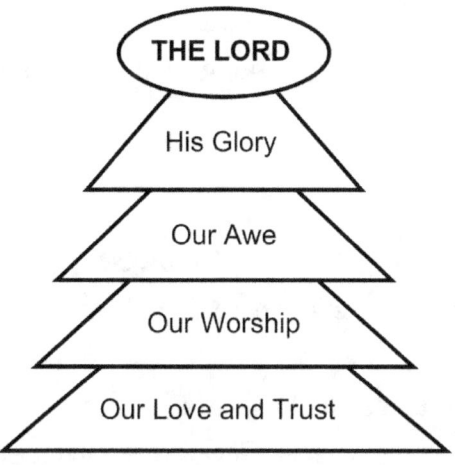

THE TREE OF AWE

Figure 14. The Tree of Awe

Years ago, Jan and I had the privilege of being part of a conference for Swiss pastors. The venue for the conference was a beautiful hotel high up in the Alps, overlooking alpine lakes. During one of the noon breaks, Jan and I took a short walk outside and found a bench next to a Swiss couple. As we talked, I mentioned how majestic the Alps were to us.

The man said, "Can I tell you a story?" He then told of a couple from the United Kingdom who were visiting Switzerland for the first time. They had heard of the Swiss Alps but wanted to see them for themselves.

They arrived at the foot of a trail that would lead them to the top of one of the Alps, but all was covered in fog. They were deeply disappointed but began to climb the trail, nevertheless. Somewhere along the way, they needed to rest, so they found a bench and sat next to the couple that Jan and I were sitting next to.

The British couple mentioned to our Swiss friends how disappointed they were in not being able to see the mountains due to the heavy fog. Then, as they were sitting together and chatting, something wonderful happened. The fog lifted, and right before them, the Alps emerged in stunning majesty. The man then said with great trembling, "It's too much! It's too much! It's too much!"

One day we will fall on our faces before Jesus in all of His glory and say, "You're too much! You're too much! You're too much!" How appropriate.

Going Deeper

Questions are *quests* toward deeper insight and better application. Individually or as a group, the following questions invite you to wade into greater depth of understanding.

- Describe a time in your life in which you trembled. What did that do to you?
- When have you been struck by awe at God?
- Of the five disciplines that lead to increased trembling, which one is most challenging to you? Why is it so challenging?
- Reread this paragraph. What strikes a chord? Why?

> The crisis of our age is that of boredom. So much of life is predictable and under our control. Thus, we vicariously seek excitement in sports, music, and sexual activity. In our digital, leisure-soaked, air-conditioned, therapeutic world, we have lost the gift of awe. Indeed, we have insulated ourselves from the terrifying, the wonderous, and the out-of-our-control forces of wind, storm, hail, and earthquake. They make us feel small and vulnerable. Vulnerability is not what we deem to be a good life, but it is for those who want to make advances in the virtue of humility.

- Which application tied to awe and trembling will you pursue this week?

Chapter 10

Helping

*"When I was a boy and I would see scary things in the news,
my mother would say to me, 'Look for the helpers.
You will always find people who are helping."*

FRED ROGERS[1]

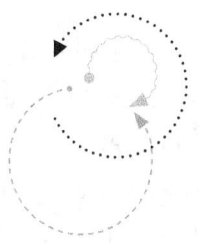

When God wanted humanity to appreciate who He was, He made a woman.

Eve was her name, given to the man as a helper (Genesis 2:20-22). A helper is someone who gives us what we cannot give ourselves. In the gift of woman to man, God gave him love, caring, intimacy, communication, and joy on a human plane. These are things the man could not have given himself. He needed a helper.

The same word that signifies the beauty of the woman as the man's helper ("help" is the Hebrew word *ezer*) is most frequently used to refer to God. *Ezer* refers to a source of strength outside of ourselves. Of the twenty-one uses of *ezer* in the Old Testament, sixteen are used of God. God gives to us that which we cannot give ourselves. What are the gifts resulting from God as Helper? Fear is banished, flourishing abounds, security pervades, and enemies are vanquished. "So do not fear, for I am with you; do not be dismayed, for I am your God. I will strengthen you and help you; I will uphold you with my righteous right hand" (Isaiah 41:10).

As we saw in chapter 8, Jesus was primarily a servant sent by the Father to serve all of us who could not save ourselves. If taking on the role of a slave was good enough for the Son of Man, it should be good enough for us. Helping is a noble venture, and as we help, we do it humbly.

It would be an easy thing to do—to help others in their need—if it weren't for us. To be honest, we often get in the way of being God's agents of blessing. Opportunity abounds. Time is not of the essence. Rather, it is we who are the blockage.

When we considered earlier what it would look like for pride to be our guide in section 1, what was apparent was that self-love, with eros at the center, was the seedbed of pride. For if we have a high estimation of ourselves, we will have a lower estimation of God and of the people around us made in His image.

The new paradigm of self, where agape is at the center, will seamlessly lead to service. The diagram below gives us a good image of what our new core of life looks like as we are connected to Christ, who is Himself agape.

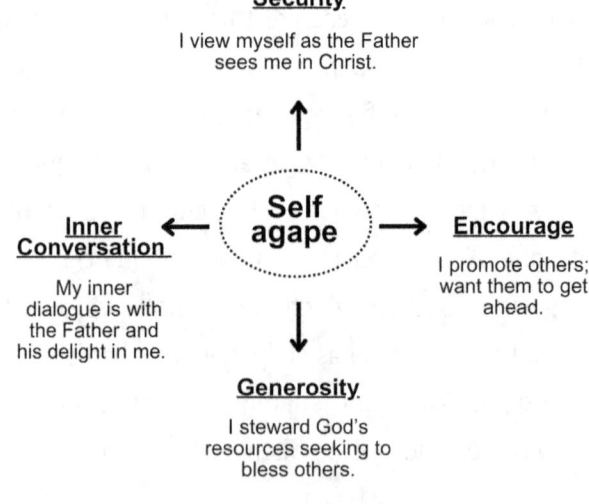

Figure 15. Self-Agape

We feel tension when the needs of others embrace the means of meeting those needs that we possess. We are conflicted. The conflict is between eros and agape. This is another way of saying the conflict lies between the self being the end or the means to the end.

Lewis Smedes had a helpful response to our tension.

There is a simple answer, I believe, though it is not easy to practice. The answer is this: our *self* can be either a *means* or an *end*. If we make ourselves the *end*, the ultimate goal, the final aim of our striving, we are in conflict with agape love. Love does not seek its self as the living end. Instead love is the power that drives us to seek our selves as a *means* to being agents of love. This will take some thinking through, and it is very important to get it straight. If we do not have it clear, we will never relieve our conflict between self-seeking and self-denial.[2]

Before we get to how to practice helping others, we need to consider some basic tenets of serving.

We need to prepare for discomfort. "No sweat, no service" might be our motto. Jesus called it suffering. He described the fruitful life as the dying life—like a seed that is set down into the earth to die (John 12:23-24). John Stott wrote, "It is not just that suffering belongs to service, but that suffering is indispensable to fruitful or effective service."[3] Discomfort is normative for all who want to advance in servanthood.

We need to deny our love of self. Following Jesus is more than putting our faith in Him and waiting to ascend to heaven. True following means death. "No death to self, no life for others" might be our motto. "Then he said to them all: 'Whoever wants to be my disciple must deny themselves and take up their cross daily and follow me. For whoever wants to save their life will lose it, but whoever loses their life for me will save it'" (Luke 9:23-24).

With these two seminal tenets in mind, discomfort and self-denial, we now move to the practical question of "Now what?" How do we do it? Follow Jesus daily by helping others daily.

EEO (Eyes and Ears Open)

We do not have to create need. It is already all around us. What is necessary is to become attentive to the many opportunities presenting themselves to us. How glorious it is to wake up every morning and say something like, "Good morning, Lord. How wonderful that You and I will be wading into a lake of neediness today! Give me ears to hear needy cries, eyes to see those in need of our help."

The parents of Fred Rogers, Nancy and Jim, were the wealthiest couple in the small town of Latrobe, in western Pennsylvania, near Pittsburgh. Fred was driven to and from school by the family chauffeur. Jim Rogers owned and ran two companies: the Latrobe Die Casting Company and the McFeely Brick Company. The Rogers were millionaires, but unpretentious and always on the lookout for those who were in need of the help that they felt called to give. "In her role as a community watchdog, [Nancy Rogers] could find out which families needed help. As often as not, the solution to a problem involved Jim and Nancy Rogers writing a check, which they did on an almost weekly basis."[4]

Fred Rogers grew up in a home that was deeply committed to Christ and to those in the community who had need. He learned early on to keep his eyes and ears open to the lack of those around him.

NTBS (Not to Be Seen)

The best way to kill pride is to do good things for others secretly. By secretly, I mean without getting caught in the act and without talking about it afterward.

In our early years of living in Germany, we bought an old upright piano that Jan joyfully played, often in preparation for leading worship in one of our churches. When we moved, the piano moved, which resulted in keys sticking and chords out of tune. We had a piano tuner come in to get the old lady back into shape. The tuner did the best he could but said there was structural damage to the piano that needed to be repaired for the piano to maintain its sound. He estimated the cost to be around five thousand deutsche marks. We simply did not have that kind of money.

The miracle happened on Easter Monday. Easter Monday is a holiday in Germany, which means no mail delivery. Our toddler, Lukas, discovered an envelope at the base of our front door, where mail is delivered through a slot, with the words "for a new piano." He brought it to us. We opened it. It was filled with fifty bills in denominations of one hundred. Five thousand deutsche marks! The money was enough to trade in our old piano and purchase a new one. We suspect it might have been Nancy Rogers. But to this day, we have no clue as to who blessed us so generously.

BS (Baby Steps)

The needs around us can at times be overwhelming, causing us to freeze and not take action. We learn that in the life of Jesus, there were many hurt and needy people. He healed some, but not all. Once He said, "The poor you will always have with you" (Mark 14:7). There will never be a day in which we wake up without people around us who cannot help themselves.

How do we navigate need without end? We do it by wading gently into the lake of lack. Like when we learn to walk, we will take baby steps. We will thereby begin to understand that success in learning to be humble begins by taking action, however little it may be. The alternative, inactivity, is simply maintaining the status quo.

For the next ten minutes, make your simple list of two or three baby steps you can take to help alleviate need today. Go to the Lord in prayer and ask Him to reveal to you who the people are that you can touch and in what way you can help them. Then take it one step at a time—one act of kindness and then another.

LOB (Living Off-Balance)

A Christian is a follower of Jesus who lives under the influence of the Holy Spirit. To be filled with the Spirit is to be directed by Him. We can only be led by the Spirit of God when we relinquish control over our lives.

There is much said and written today about balanced living, a concept foreign to Christianity. God does not want us to be in control of our lives; rather, He wants to be in control of our lives. This means that we will give up our perfectionistic tendencies and learn to live in the clutter that is real life. In following Jesus, we do not make plans and then ask God to bless them. Rather, we put ourselves under the leadership of Jesus and ask Him to direct our steps. This will inevitably lead to living off-center and off-balance. And that is good.

The emotional state of learning humility will entail feeling disjointed. To be out of step, but in step with the Spirit of God (Galatians 5:25) is good. It means we are walking by faith. And sometimes, that walk feels strange, like being out of kilter.

QBS (Question-Based Service)

For years, I have been trying to lead conversations by asking a person, "How are you?" Whatever their response, I come back with, "Tell me more." This is an invitation to go deep, to unpack life, and to honestly divulge how one is doing. More often than not, "tell me more" has surfaced as personal turbulence or unrest. That's when I pray for courage and ask if I can pray for them on the spot.

A friend of mine was once the senior pastor of a very large church. They had five services on the weekend and planted a new church every year. Thousands of people came, and many were there because of the wonderful, gifted preaching of my friend. After the service, people would come up to him with their comments and, sometimes, criticisms. He told me that in every encounter, he would ask, "How can I help you?" Wow! When was the last time someone asked us, "How can I help you?" My friend had an administrative assistant standing next to him during such moments. The job of the assistant was to write down the need and the contact information of the petitioner and then find a way of having the need met. But that would not have happened had my friend not asked, "How can I help you?"

Suppose we would seek to ask one person each day, "How can I help you?" Imagine the difference it would make in the lives of those around us. And imagine how we would be transformed into servants and helpers. We may not have all the resources to meet every need, and sometimes we will be God's conduits, connecting them with others who would help, but many would be aided.

COW (Cup of Water)

Most of us do not find ourselves in the financially privileged position of Jim and Nancy Rogers. We simply can't write a check and alleviate need. In fact, many of us are just trying to make it from month to month, paycheck to paycheck.

When helping others, it's not about the amount given but the action of giving. Jesus emphasized this. "Truly I tell you, anyone who gives you a cup of water in my name because you belong to the Messiah will certainly not lose their reward" (Mark 9:41). In the economy of the Messiah, it's the little things—quite unspectacular—given to needy people that become major.

Our neighbor in Frankfurt, Germany, was dying of the ravages of cancer. My wife, Jan, was by her side until she died. Jan, who was sleeping on a mattress on the floor of the living room next to our neighbor's hospital bed, woke up very early in the morning. She went over to our friend, spoke lovingly to her, caressed her hair, and then moistened her lips with a wet sponge. For the past five days, our friend Sibylle had neither eaten, drunk, nor spoken.

On numerous occasions, Jan had shared the gospel with Sibylle, but each time with a disappointing response. On this morning, after wetting her chapped lips, Jan quietly said to Sibylle, "You can trust Jesus." Our friend opened her eyes and said, "I trust Him." Those were her last words.

Jan's service to Sibylle was a mattress, a dampened sponge, a caress, and words of loving care. Cup-of-Water serving is never spectacular but always welcome. It's goodness that comes just in time.

LIH (Listening Is Helping)

Our culture has an army of capable people in the service industry to meet our needs. All we need to do is phone and food will be delivered, the house cleaned, the car serviced, the grass cut, or the snow shoveled. But there is a service that many people around us need more than practical help, and it is for someone to listen to them.

Listening is loving. If we have honestly listened to someone without an agenda, they have felt love. Anyone can listen, but few do it. Why? Because they have not been trained to listen. We would rather talk than listen. The skill of listening demands that we ourselves take a back seat to the person across from us. We purposefully neglect self-interest and show interest in others. "How are you doing? Tell me more" is a great way to start us on the journey of listening.

Fred Rogers had this knack, and it made him so attractive. "Whenever one sat down to talk with him, urgency seemed to dissipate, discussion proceeded at a measured, almost otherworldly pace, and the deepest feelings and thoughts were given patient attention."[5]

Listening is loving. What a difference honest attention to the other would make in the depth of our marital relationship, in our work at the office, or in our relationships with our children. To listen, we need to cultivate the discipline of intentionality, seeking to listen to others and focus on their world. Such discipline will require us to throttle down our instinctive desire to have conversations about us.

WI (Welcome Interruptions)

I remember years ago going with a colleague to the hospital to visit a person in one of our churches in Germany. While we were visiting with this elderly woman who was recovering from her operation, she told us of a young woman that she had met who was dying of cancer and had three little children. Our friend told us of her conversations with this young mother and of her openness to the Bible and spiritual matters. My colleague and I prayed with our congregant, said goodbye to her, and left her hospital room.

What happened next still haunts me to this day. It ranks among the top five things in my life that I wish I could do over. I exited the room and looked into the room across the hall—and looked directly into the eyes of the young woman of whom we had just spoken. Her eyes were filled with pain and death. We made eye contact. Her eyes held a piercing pleading. At that moment, it was as if the Holy Spirit said to me, "Dietrich, go and talk to that woman about the hope that is within you! Her time is short."

What did I do? I suppressed the prompting. By suppressing the prompting of God, I missed out on the *kairos,* or "the right time" of God for both the dying woman and me. Oh, how I wish I could have that moment back.

May I be totally honest? I don't want my comfort to be disturbed. I'm much like the prophet Jonah, who got ticked when the shade that had grown over him to protect him from the burning sun was gone.

We remember the story. Jonah was wilting under the Middle Eastern sun. God provided a vine to grow up to shade Jonah from the oppressive heat. Then God sent a worm to gnaw at the root of the vine, and the vine died. Jonah was beside himself with anger. His comfort had been divinely disturbed. And he didn't like it (Jonah 4).

God's message to him was this: Jonah, you are more concerned about your personal comfort than about the eternal state of thousands of people below you.

Can I ask this question: How are you doing when your physical comfort is disturbed? Either you can get angry and sulk, like Jonah did, or you can view discomfort as a messenger sent by God to convey a deeper significance: the condition of lost people means more to God than my comfort.

Both the comfort of the vine and the discomfort brought upon its demise are provisions sent by God. When God blesses you, rejoice. When God takes away your comfort, rejoice. There is something more important in this world than our sense of well-being.

One of our greatest challenges is that of our expectations. In the Greek world, there are two words that speak of time. The one word is *chronos*, from which we derive English words such as *chronology*, *chronic, chronograph,* and *chronicle. Chronos* denotes what we expect to happen according to our schedules. Our calendars, Day-Timers, vacation planning, and jobs around the house are all predicated on our schedule. *Chronos* is the intentional, measured, thought-out, anticipated, and linear use of our time. *Chronos* is what we expect to happen because we have planned for it in advance.

The other Greek term for time is *kairos*. At the beginning of His ministry, Jesus said, "The time [*kairos*] has come . . . the kingdom of God has come near. Repent and believe the good news!" (Mark 1:15). When Jesus talked about the separation of the wheat and the tares on judgment day, He referred to *kairos* "at that time," (Matthew 13:30).

Kairos also refers to God's appointed time. What is on God's agenda for us, *kairos*, is often not what is on our agenda for ourselves, *chronos*. Here's the rub: God's *kairos* will often collide with our *chronos*. What we have planned for the day will be interrupted by what God has planned for us that day.

God is challenging us to be interrupted, to allow our *chronos* to be broken into by God's *kairos*. So much of what God wants to do through us is situational in nature. We learn to respond positively to the interruptions God sends our way. We should not be surprised when God interrupts our plans to do something greater than what was on our agenda.

Our journey on the path of greater humility starts every day anew. It is in the morning, when the day is fresh, clean, and untrodden, that we anticipate what awaits us. This is when we often plan our day, make our to-do lists, and set our goals to accomplish great and less-than-great things.

The morning hour could become our hour of surrender to the greater plans that God has for us—plans to bless others through actively helping them in their need. We will anticipate not being in full control, living a bit off-balanced, welcoming interruptions, being attentive to what we see and hear, and listening for the turbulence beneath the lies of "I'm fine. I'm okay." And as we begin to humbly serve others in new and beautiful ways, sometimes costly to us, we will hear the voice of the Father break through to our hearts, saying, "Well done, good and faithful servant! You have been faithful with a few things; I will put you in charge of many things. Come and share your master's happiness!" (Matthew 25:21).

Going Deeper

Questions are *quests* toward deeper insight and better application. Individually or as a group, the following questions invite you to wade into greater depth of understanding.

- Who has helped you lately, and what did that look like?
- Look at Figure 15 "Self-Agape." Which of the four descriptions of sacrificial love is strongest in your life? Which is weakest?
- Reread this passage. How have you embraced discomfort in serving others as normative?

- How have you embraced discomfort in serving others as normative?

  John Stott wrote, "It is not just that suffering belongs to service, but that suffering is indispensable to fruitful, effective service." Discomfort is normative for all who want to advance in servanthood.

- This chapter lists eight ways in which we can become better servants. Which of the eight is most challenging to you and why?
- What would it mean for you to step out of your comfort zone this week and serve others? How would you do that practically?

Chapter 11

Discerning

"The unexamined life is not worth living."
SOCRATES[1]

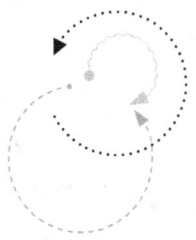

Michael Plant was a legend among yacht-racing enthusiasts. Three times, Plant had circumnavigated the globe on sailing vessels, often facing innumerable perils brought on by gale-force storms, monstrous waves, and mechanical failure. Plant was on his way to Les Sables-d'Olonne, France, in October 1992, for the start of the Vendée Globe Challenge, a 24,000-mile nonstop solo race around the world.

Alas, Michael Plant's state-of-the-art sixty-foot racing sloop, *Coyote*, lost radio contact less than two weeks before the race was to commence. The United States Coast Guard, along with the Navy, deployed planes to search for the forty-two-year-old U.S. seasoned sailor.

A Liberian registered tanker, the *Protank Orinoco*, spotted the capsized yacht and radioed the United States Coast Guard. *Coyote*'s hull was discovered floating in an area about 500 miles north of the Azores, an island chain in the mid-Atlantic.

What was remarkable about the sighting of the *Coyote* was that its

143

8,400-pound ballast bulb secured to the bottom of the hull was missing. The ballast gave the boat the needed weight to right itself in even the fiercest of storms. Without it, the boat was doomed. Michael Plant was never found but probably drowned when the *Coyote* capsized.[2]

The most important part of a sailing vessel lies beneath the surface of the water. The same principle applies to human beings as well.

Much of our lives are lived above the surface of the waterline. Above the surface is where we find our activities—working, recreating, friendships, scheduling, producing, and fretting. Shallowness of life is directly related to living exclusively above the waterline. If we want depth, we need to get below the surface to open ourselves up to the inner exploration of the labyrinth inside us, which is the heart.

On our journey to becoming people of humble disposition, what comes after trembling and helping? It is discerning. Discerning is taking a deep dive into the universe of our thoughts, motives, longings, frustrations, joys, fears, and personal histories.

We are amiss when we think that we know ourselves well. What we know are the things on the surface of our lives—our schedules, the people we have met, our financial situation, and the many tasks to be done. Why does David in Psalm 139 ask God to search his heart? "Search me, God, and know my heart; test me and know my anxious thoughts. See if there is any offensive way in me, and lead me in the way everlasting" (Psalm 139:23-24). The reason David asked God to reveal his innermost thoughts and motives is because David was unaware of them. We, like David, often live as if the under-the-water part of us does not exist.

The other day, I was praying the David prayer of discernment. Specifically, I honed into "see if there is any offensive way in me." That night, I woke up at about 12:30 a.m. and went to the bathroom, where my iPhone was. The day before, I had been keenly following an investment that I had made and wanted to know how it was faring. Having looked at the price action of my investment perhaps twenty times that day, one might suspect a slight addiction. But what did I do in the early hours of a new day? I turned on my phone and looked at the upsurge in the value of my investment. I went back to bed happy.

As soon as I stretched out on my bed, the Holy Spirit spoke, not audibly yet plainly unmistakably. He said something like, "Dietrich, why is it that when you turned on your phone, you did not instinctively search for a word from Me but instead sought out a capricious integer?" (Okay, I'm not sure He used the exact phrase "a capricious integer," but I got the message). He went on, "You have made an idol out of a means to an end. You have set your heart on vapor."

I was smitten. I knew the Spirit of God had answered my prayer. The offensive thing was revealed to me. I repented and asked for forgiveness. Then I sensed Him saying, "Dietrich, you are my beloved. You have no need to feed your soul with such sawdust. I am enough and more than enough. I satisfy all of your longings." That's when I savored being near the heart of my Father, blissfully falling back into a deep sleep.

Plummeting the Depths of the Heart— The Goal of Discerning

Remember the most frequent lie many of us tell daily? "I'm fine." We have learned the fine art of covering up who we really are and how we are truly doing. Perhaps the art of deception is congenital, given to us at birth and passed on to us by our original ancestors, Adam and Eve. After they had eaten the fruit from the tree of the knowledge of good and evil, "the eyes of both of them were opened, and they realized they were naked" (Genesis 3:7). Then they went about sewing fig leaves together to literally cover up their guilt and shame. They did not want God to know what they knew.

The word *discerning* originated in Latin and means "to separate," as in, to separate kernels of wheat from chaff. When we discern, we are trying to distinguish between who we really are and what is untrue about who we have become. The process of distinguishing between truth and error is also known as confessing. Confessing is agreeing with God as to how He sees us. The Apostle John wrote, "If we confess our sins, he is faithful and just and will forgive us our sins and purify us from all unrighteousness" (1 John 1:9).

Theologian Lewis Smedes told us that knowing is directly related to discerning.

> Discernment is the ability to see the difference between things. It is the power to see what is really happening, to see what is really important and what is not important. Discernment is insight—the power to see *inside* of things. It is the strange and subtle ability to see beneath the surface, to sense the personal factors of any situation, and to grasp what spiritual issues are really at stake. When we are directly involved, discernment is an insight into the mixture of motives moving our own hearts. Working its way through real life, love needs the gift of discernment to focus its drive toward others in helping service.[3]

The great French Cistercian monk Bernard of Clairvaux put his finger on what it is that we are after when we seek discernment. "If you examine yourself inwardly by the light of truth and without dissimulation, and judge yourself without flattery; no doubt you will be humbled in your own eyes, becoming contemptible in your own sight as a result of this true knowledge of yourself."[4]

The "true knowledge of yourself" is what we are after when we ask God to help us discern how well we are humbly walking with our God (Micah 6:8).

On the Path of Discernment

But how do we do it? How do we actually learn the craft of looking beneath the surface of things to discover who we really are and what we want others to know about us?

Invitation

As David did, we too begin the journey to greater knowledge of self by inviting the Lord of our lives, who knows what is in man (John 2:25), to share His knowledge with us. We pray with David, "Investigate my life, O God, find out everything about me; Cross-examine and test me, get a clear picture of what I'm about; see for yourself whether I've done anything wrong—then guide me on the road to eternal life" (Psalm 139:23-24, MSG).

For those of us who know ourselves to be in the family of God through Jesus Christ, we invite the Father to reveal our thoughts and motives to us because we are safe in His love. If it weren't so, we would fear anything negative the Lord might reveal to us. It would come across as damning. Instead, we invite Him to search our hearts out of deep gratitude for being accepted and loved by Him.

The invitation extended to God to search our thoughts, motives, desires, and actions can be formulated in a simple prayer such as this: "Father God, thank You for the gift of being known by You and of being accepted by You into Your very heart. I know You love me. But, to be honest, I often do not know myself. I therefore invite You to uncover the fig leaves I have constructed. Show me my false motives, my unfounded anxiety, my hurtful words and actions, my desire to disengage with people instead of loving them, my tendency to want to look good, my exaggerating accounts, and my secret loves. Thank You. Amen."

Silence

God reveals deeper things when we stop talking. Silence is the bridge upon which the Lord transports insight. Again, David helped us here. "Be still, and know that I am God" (Psalm 46:10). *Know* is the same word for sexual intimacy: to know one's marital partner. God longs to be intimate with us, revealing who He is and who we are in His presence.

For several years now, I have been purposefully repenting. One hour of every month is my practice. I begin by praying the prayer that David prayed in Psalm 139:23-24 about searching my heart. I am kneeling and have before me a blank piece of paper and a pen. After I pray, inviting God to help me discern what is in me, I listen. It may take five minutes or ten, or even fifteen. Inevitably, He speaks.

I remember one spring day doing this exercise in the Jewish cemetery in Frankfurt, a twenty-minute walk from where we lived. A cemetery is a quiet place in which to be quiet. I have learned that I need such quiet places if I want to hear Him. I was totally surprised at what I heard that day: "Heed Jan" was what I distinctly heard the Lord say to my spirit. Even Jan was surprised when I told her what God had revealed to me. And she was happy.

Why did God tell me to "heed Jan"? Well, maybe it was because I wasn't paying attention to her—what she said, how she felt, what she longed for. If it had not been for the kindness of God, I never would have come up with such a startling message.

Interconnectedness

Discernment means we are going about the business of connecting the dots between our outer and inner worlds. We want to see the correlation between what is above and what is below the surface of our lives. The "desert fathers referred to such interconnectedness as *theoria physike*—a vision of how things hang together."

Henri Nouwen elaborated on what this is and how to attain it.

Perceiving, seeing through, understanding, and being aware of God's presence are what is meant by discernment. Opening the heart to what is really and truly "there" is a fruit of contemplation and spiritual practice. Those who practice discernment are often more contemplative than those who are so active that they do not take the time to reflect on the inner meaning of appearances.[5]

What keeps us from the work of contemplation is our activity and our busyness. I remember, as a young follower of Christ, riding in the passenger seat with my friend Pastor Mike Frans. On the dashboard right in front of me, Mike had taped a phrase that initially startled me: "Beware of the Barrenness of Busyness." I have often lingered over that phrase. Sometimes the work that God wants to do within us gets annihilated by the work that we do for God. If, in doing the work of God, we leave out being silent before God and waiting on Him, we should not be surprised when our production is vapid.

We are often guilty of spuddling. According to the Oxford English Dictionary, *spuddle* is an old English term meaning "to be extremely busy whilst achieving absolutely nothing." We were made for more than to be busy.

Interconnectedness is the result of the capaciousness of the heart. To be capacious is to have plenty of room—a spacious and roomy place in the heart—for God to do His voluminous work of uncovering.

Again, Nouwen clarified.

This wonderful story about seeing through to the heart of things raises a deeper question: Do I want to be fully seen by Jesus? Do I want to be known by him? If I do, then a faith can grow that will open my eyes to heaven and reveal Jesus as the Son of God. I will see great things when I am willing to be seen. I will receive new eyes that can see the mysteries of God's own life, but only when I allow God to see me, all of me, even those parts that I myself do not want to see.

While I was at the Abbey of the Genesee, I found that my anger and my desire to be special and to be admired all bubbled up in my times of solitude. I began to see how in so many ways I had been living for my own glory rather than for the greater glory of God.[6]

Interconnectedness is not shy in enlisting the help of others. Sometimes I ask my fellow sojourners if they would like to become more like Jesus. Inevitably, they say, "Of course." Then I ask them to do something extremely courageous. I tell them to go to three people who know them well and, in the coming week, ask them all the same question: If you were God and had the power to change anything about who I am, what would that be?

After they engage in three such courageous conversations, we meet to talk about the answers they have gathered. Usually, all three responses from their friends flow in the same direction. The answers given are the touchpoints of humility, for they reveal the areas that Jesus wants to lovingly change for more of Jesus to be seen in them.

The Purpose and Goal of Discerning

To what end do we seek God to open up to us the abyss of our hearts? The goal is to know God and, in knowing Him, to be struck by how far we are from being like Him. Not only that, but as we gaze upon the great chasm that separates us from Him, we are immediately smitten by knowing that we are loved by Him beyond our wildest dreams. Though the character gap between us and God is a mile wide, His love for us is so intimate to not let an atom come between His heart and ours.

Discernment reveals new priorities, directions, and gifts from God. We come to realize that what previously seemed so important for our lives, loses its power over us. Our desire to be successful, well liked, and influential becomes increasingly less important as we come closer to God's heart. To our surprise, we even may experience a strange inner freedom to follow a new call or direction as previous concerns move into the background of our consciousness. We begin to see the beauty of the small and hidden life that Jesus lived in Nazareth. Most rewarding of all is the discovery that as we pray more each day, God's will—that is, God's concrete ways of loving us and our world—gradually is made known to us.[7]

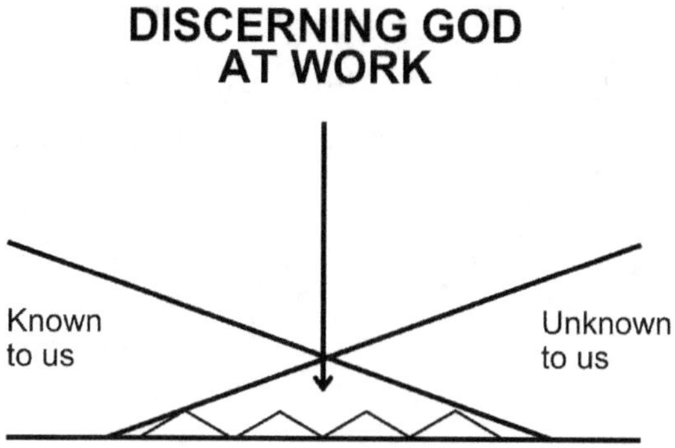

**DISCERNING GOD
AT WORK**

Known
to us

Unknown
to us

Figure 16. Discerning God at Work

In going from the known to the unknown, we need the help of the Holy Spirit, who searches "the deep things of God" (1 Corinthians 2:10). Often blind to our own foibles and cover-ups, we desperately need the detective work of God in our hearts. His is a work of love, even as He uncovers that which is unlovely.

The most important feature of a sailboat is that which remains unseen—the ballast that hides under the water's surface. The most important part of being human is not what people perceive of us, but that which God sees—the unseen heart. Courageous discernment is the gift of God that leads us into deeper and abiding humility.

Going Deeper

Questions are *quests* toward deeper insight and better application. Individually or as a group, the following questions invite you to wade into greater depth of understanding.

- Have you discovered something about who you are that is relatively new to you? What would that be?
- Michael Plant's boat had a balanced bulb that was designed to keep his vessel from sinking. What is the unseen weight in your soul that is keeping you from sinking?

- Under "On the Path of Discernment," what is a discipline that is most difficult for you to do? (Do it this week).
- How have you allowed God to plummet the deep secret chambers of your heart?
- What is it that you need to repent of?

Chapter 12

Progressing

"What matters, what Heaven desires and Hell fears, is precisely that further step; out of our depth, out of our own control."

C. S. LEWIS[1]

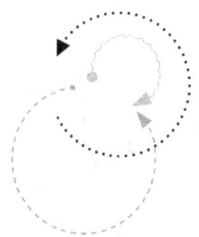

I look out of my study window and follow the progression of a tree's growth in the neighbor's yard. In the spring, I see green buds on gray branches; signs of life and hope. In the summer, those branches are hidden by a blanket of lush green leaves, which produce small red berries, proof of abundance on which birds feast. Now in the fall, the leaves are turning orange, yellow, and red—fire for the eyes. In a month, when winter has entered the neighborhood, the leaves will have fallen, leaving the tree ashen and barren, waiting again for spring.

I am that tree. Spring and summer have passed, and now fall is upon me. With the cold and dampness, there is a penultimate beauty that only comes in the fall; it's the time to reflect and record what spring and summer have brought. In the fall stage of life, there is nothing to prove, yet much to savor. Perhaps there will be a winter, but if so, it is still a ways off in the distance.

For a long time, during the spring and part of the summer of my life, I thought that the things I did (ministry) were the most important. They were not. Sometimes the greatest enemy of Christian ministry is the ministry itself, for it can become idolatry. I have repented of that.

Are we in our spring? Or in our summer? Perhaps, like me, we are in the fall of our lives, or possibly the winter. Regardless of what season we find ourselves in, what is most important is the growth (or non-growth) that our lives are evidencing. Learning to live humbly has much to do with personal spiritual growth and progressing on our journey of becoming more like Jesus.

Consider the following diagram, which I have labeled "The Growth Scale." The Apostle Paul endured great pain—birth pangs—in his desire to see Christ formed in the believers who were part of the churches he planted in Galatia. "The Growth Scale" lays out for us three possible descriptions of how Christ is being formed in us: progressing, stagnating, or declining in Christlikeness. It is important that we assess where we see ourselves on "The Growth Scale." Are we progressing, stagnating, or declining in our walk with Jesus?

Learning humility will entail a life of steady progression—not perfection, but progress. When IRS agents are trained to uncover fake U.S. dollar bills, they are drilled on noticing the details on government-authorized money. They do not spend much time on counterfeit money. When these agents are well acquainted with the details of official bills, detecting falsehood is easy. Thus, it will be for us; we will not spend much time looking at stagnation or decline, as they are self-explanatory, but will look at what it would mean to lead a life of growth or progression in the Christian life.

Figure 17. The Growth Scale

What Progressing in Christlikeness Looks Like
Relishing God's Word

Perhaps the prophet Jeremiah had just enjoyed a sumptuous meal, exquisite taste lingering on his memory palette when he penned these words: "When your words came, I ate them; they were my joy and my heart's delight" (Jeremiah 15:16). Joy is what is ours when we commune with God over His Word.

Many metaphors describe God's Word in its freshness, power, beauty, and truth to guide us:

The Bible is a fire that burns away all of the dross of our lives.

It is a sledgehammer that breaks down evil barriers.
(Jeremiah 23:29)

It is honey, sweet to the taste, inviting more of the same.
(Proverbs 16:24)

It is mother's milk that sustains and allows for growth.
(1 Peter 2:2)

It is a sword that cuts so precisely, exposing our inner world.
(Ephesians 6:17)

It is a seed from which goodness flourishes. (1 Peter 1:23)

It is a mirror that lets us see who we really are. (James 1:23)

But above all of these, the Bible, as a meeting place between us and God Himself, is "my joy and my heart's delight." It is so for those who are making progress in their Christian lives. Though the mind is engaged when we read the Bible, ultimately it is the heart that is stirred. We savor its truth because we, in turn, savor friendship with the God of truth.

Why is it that far too many Christians, when they open the Bible and begin to read, feel nothing? It's like standing at home plate, swinging, and missing as the ball comes whizzing past us. Sometimes, it comes down to not knowing how to go on a date with God. Joy-filled Bible reading is like dating. The thrill of being with someone we like, or love, is enhanced by the anticipation we have before the date. Enjoying friendship with God in Bible reading has much to do with anticipation. He is waiting to love on us. Are we expecting to be embraced and surprised by being immersed in love with the God of the universe?

Jean Pierre de Caussade, a Jesuit priest and spiritual director to many in eighteenth-century France, conveyed to us his insight into how to read the Bible for more than intellectual gain. "Fix your attention upon what you are reading, and do not think upon what follows. . . . Pause now and then to give these glad truths time to soak more thoroughly into your soul and to make easier the workings of the Holy Spirit. . . . Let the words penetrate the heart rather than the mind."[2]

Over the years, I have found that I need to prepare my heart in anticipation of meeting with the Champion of my soul in His Word. "No Bible, no breakfast" has been my motto from the time I was eighteen years old. By saturating my heart in the Word of God, my day is anchored.

The ACTS exercise has been a simple yet profoundly valuable help. Before I open up my Bible, I write out four short sentences that serve to prime the pump of my heart.

- *Adoration* is first. I praise God for one of His attributes or character qualities.
- *Confession* is when I note what I have done or thought that saddened His heart.
- *Thanksgiving* is registering my gratitude for what He has provided for me and others.
- *Supplication* is a petition that I bring to the Lord, asking Him to fulfill it and, in so doing, glorify His name.

Another exercise has been helpful in savoring God's Word, sucking on it as we would do with fine Swiss chocolate. When our neighbor, Alexander, came to Christ during our church plant in Mannheim, Germany, I met with him in his office at home twice weekly, Tuesdays and Thursdays before work. For a year, we read the Psalms together and prayed over them.

But before we began our time together, I gave Alexander two colored pencils, one red and one green. I instructed him to underline any promise that God made in the Psalms with the green pencil. Any attribute of God was underlined with the red pencil. After a year of doing this, Alexander had his own mini-theology of the person and the promises of God in the Psalms. What a rich treasure trove of truth and beauty!

Retreating with God

When we look at the life of Jesus, we discover how often He went on retreats to be alone with the Father. Before He began His public ministry, He was led into the desert for forty days of fasting to marinate His soul in fellowship with the Father. Jesus was offering us a pattern to follow.

Jesus was at home in the presence of His Father, and the Father was at home with Jesus. At Jesus' baptism, which marked the beginning of His public ministry, those present apparently heard the intimate words of God the Father: "You are my Son, whom I love; with you I am well pleased" (Mark 1:11). Jesus often sought times and places where He could be alone with His Father and enjoy communion with Him. "In the morning, while it was still very dark, he got up and went out to a deserted place, and there he prayed" (Mark 1:35, NRSVA). After days of exhausting ministry, Jesus sought out His Father's company (Mark 6:46; Mark 9:7). Before the single greatest test He would ever face—His execution on the cross—He went to a grove of olive trees and prayed, "Abba, Father . . ." (Mark 14:36). *Abba* is an Aramaic term of endearment, a loving, intimate word for father, used by young children. Jesus breathed intimacy with His Father as we breathe oxygen. That intimacy was the source of His greatest joy and the strength behind everything He did.

This thirst for God, a deep longing more intense than a baby's longing for its mother's milk, motivates us as it did Jesus. Jesus could never get enough of His Father. In the same way, an ever-present desire to be in the presence of the Father and in close fellowship with Him must always be the starting point for those of us who want to make progress in being more like Christ. In the face of our greatest successes or our worst defeats, we find deep contentment in the presence of our Father.

The enemy of retreating with God is our schedule. What, therefore, is needed is to purposely schedule mini-retreats with the Lord during the day. Perhaps we can do this very simply by attaching a fifteen-minute time frame to our daily meals, either before or after them.

What to do on our mini-retreats? Think of chocolate (or any other delightful food). What if we were to savor the Father in the same way we savor Swiss chocolate? We would mentally latch onto one aspect of who He has shown Himself to be in His Word, perhaps something we read that morning in our Bible reading. We would then sit with that truth or attribute and turn it over and over in our minds, relishing it. We would then turn our meditation into prayer to the Father, thanking Him for it and telling Him how much we want to live it out in our lives.

Gladly Obeying

In the Lord's Prayer, we request, "Your will be done on earth *as* it is in heaven" (Matthew 6:10, emphasis mine). How is the will of the Lord done in heaven by angels? Every time an angel gets an assignment from the Father, he excitedly leaps up and does that assignment joyfully, fully, and immediately. For angels, obedience is an act of joy. It should be for us as well.

Remember the story of the paralytic in Mark chapter 2, who was carried to Jesus by his four friends while lying on a mat? His friends were both loyal to him and ingenious in the way they showed their love. The house in which Jesus was staying was packed to the gills. "There was no room left, not even outside the door" (Mark 2:2). Jesus was practically inaccessible to even a healthy person, let alone to one who could not walk. What to do? The lame man's friends came up with a bold plan. They would carry their friend up to the roof of the house, determine approximately where Jesus was teaching inside, and uncover the roof tiles, thereby fashioning an opening through which they would lower their friend into the presence of Jesus. That must have been an extensive opening, requiring time and exertion to be big enough for a grown man to fit through it.

Whereas the homeowner was contemplating using his catastrophic house insurance policy, Jesus was delighted. The text tells us, "When

Jesus *saw their faith*, he said to the paralyzed man, 'Son, your sins are forgiven. . . . I tell you, get up, take your mat and go home.'" (Mark 2:5, 11, emphasis mine).

Faith can be seen. Faith is seen in action. What we truly believe is demonstrated in how we behave. The four friends of the paralytic believed Jesus could heal him, and they acted on it. Jesus was impressed.

How does Jesus see our faith today? He sees it in the way we act on His teachings. Faith and faithfulness are related, with one leading to the other. We learned these as children in Sunday school. Remember singing:

> When we walk with the Lord in the light of His Word
> What a glory He sheds on our way!
> While we do His good will, He abides with us still
> And with all who will trust and obey.
>
> Trust and obey, for there's no other way
> To be happy in Jesus, but to trust and obey.
>
> Not a shadow can rise, not a cloud in the skies,
> But His smile quickly drives it away;
> Not a doubt or a fear, not a sigh or a tear,
> Can abide while we trust and obey.
>
> Trust and obey, for there's no other way
> To be happy in Jesus, but to trust and obey.
> Then in fellowship sweet we will sit at His feet,
> Or we'll walk by His side in the way;
> What He says we will do; where He sends, we will go,
> Never fear, only trust and obey.
>
> Trust and obey, for there's no other way
> To be happy in Jesus, but to trust and obey.[3]

'Tis so sweet to trust in Jesus
And to take Him at His word;
Just to rest upon His promise,
And to know, "Thus saith the Lord."

Jesus, Jesus, how I trust Him!
How I've proved Him o'er and o'er!
Jesus, Jesus, precious Jesus!
O for grace to trust Him more![4]

Conduct a faith analysis. At the end of the day, write down all the activities you did. Then go through them, marking each activity with either an F (for faith) or an N (for non-faith). When we do this, we discover how much or how little our day was filled with trusting Jesus, as seen in our actions. Look for patterns of both faith and non-faith. What challenges do you see God laying before you? Progression in Christlikeness is seen in owning our non-faith actions and transforming them into faith-filled actions.

Eagerly Serving

The lovely Jan gets high marks in his category. Almost anytime my wife perceives a need, she begins to think about how she can be a part of alleviating that need. I must confess that I am far from her axiomatic behavior (but I'm in training).

A mark of spiritual maturity that I look for in people is a willingness to serve. Jesus came "not to be served, but to serve" (Mark 10:45). Dietrich Bonhoeffer, in his important work *The Cost of Discipleship*, talked about two different kinds of grace. Cheap grace is that grace that we bestow on ourselves that comes from believing in Jesus but without following Him. Costly grace, however, is believing in Jesus and showing that belief by following Him.[5]

The quote at the beginning of this chapter from C. S. Lewis is about costly grace. "What matters, what Heaven desires and Hell fears, is precisely that further step; out of our depth, out of our control." We will always be out of control and out of our depth when we follow Jesus. This is good. When we find ourselves in over our heads, we allow Him to shape us. We will not live balanced lives as a result but will be off-balance. Jesus will invariably take us to people, and those people will have both small and great needs. He will then lead us to serve them.

Again, assess your life at the end of a normal day. How much of what you did was serving in the name of Jesus, being His hands, feet, eyes, and ears? Where do you see room for growth?

Telling It Like It Is

Spiritual progress is made when three things converge: relational nearness, openness, and accountability. Accountability is the courage to honestly report to someone else the way we actually lived last week. Notice that accountability in its essence is about what happened in the past tense, not present or future tense. Saying to someone that we would like to live a certain way is not conducive to growth. Growth begins to take place when we tell someone how we have actually lived—past tense.

We are talking about confessing. "Therefore confess your sins to each other and pray for each other so that you may be healed" (James 5:16). The word *confession* essentially means to tell it like it is. James said this is part of the healing process.

Yesterday, I was talking with a friend. I asked him how he was doing. He courageously opened up to me. His wife had moved out and rented an apartment. She wants out of the marriage and is resistant to counseling. He told me of his own journey in seeking out a counselor and how he has seen things in his behavior toward his wife that led to her actions. My friend is making progress in his walk with Jesus. He is telling it like it is.

Who is the person close to you that you are telling it like it is? If you want to make progress in being more like Christ, this special friend is worth her weight in gold.

When I was a student at Columbia Bible College (now Columbia International University), I recall one evening when the dean of men asked us to gather in the dorm lobby for a meeting. This was unscheduled and inopportune. The dean thought sixty young men should meet a missionary who would be speaking in the chapel that week, Dr. Helen Roseveare. The dean introduced her to us, telling us that she had been a medical missionary in the Belgian Congo from 1953 to 1973 and that she had a story to tell. He asked us if we had any questions for Dr. Roseveare.

Dr. Roseveare was a medical doctor who, as a young woman, would assess every opportunity for advancement with the question, "Is it worth it?" Is it worth taking that class at Oxford? Is it worth dating him? Is it worth taking on that speaking assignment?

To this day, I still think that the guy who asked the first question was paid. He stood up, dressed in a faded T-shirt and shorts, and said, "Dr. Roseveare, we here at Columbia Bible College often hear missionaries tell us how hard it is to serve Christ. What have you ever *suffered* for Christ on the mission field?"

We were stunned by what happened next. Slight of frame, white of hair, little Dr. Helen Roseveare responded quietly, "Well, during the Congo uprising, I was raped and tied to a tree naked. The rebels burned down the hospital that I built, and then, before my eyes, they burned the only manuscript of a book that I was writing on God's work in the Congo."

She told us that while naked and tied to a tree, watching her life's work go up in flames, the Lord spoke to her. "Helen, all of these years you have been asking the wrong question. It is not 'Is it worth it?' but 'Am I worth it?'"

What have you ever suffered for Christ? In what ways are you willing to be inconvenienced in order for God to work through you to bring about His glory and produce beautiful growth in Christlikeness?

Going Deeper

Questions are *quests* toward deeper insight and better application. Individually or as a group, the following questions invite you to wade into greater depth of understanding.

- If your life were a season (fall, winter, spring, summer), what season are you in? How can you tell?
- Look at "The Growth Scale" (Figure 17). Where would you place yourself: growing, stagnating, declining?
- What one area, if you were to address it, would lead to a perceptible updraft of your life?
- In Mark chapter 2, Jesus saw the faith of the lame man. Ask someone close to you in what ways they see your faith. How do you see your faith in action?
- What is one thing that you will do differently as a result of this chapter?

Chapter 13

Celebrating

"My fruit grows on other people's trees."
Bob Buford[1]

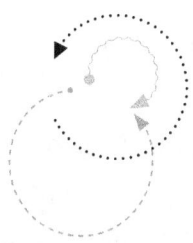

One of the greatest gifts we can give people is the gift of encouragement.

Encouragement is a power. It is a power that overcomes our desire to give up. With encouragement, we can finish high school, work grinding twelve-hour days, stay with people we love in difficult times, and achieve great feats like climbing mountains. Encouragement does so much for us, yet it's often hard to come by.

The reality is that if encouragement were our main source of nourishment, then many of us would be starving right now. Why is that? Because encouragement, praise, thanks, and recognition are the main sources of nourishment for human souls. Without them, we shrivel up inside and become bitter, nagging, and unpleasant for those around us.

"Encourage one another" is what we read in Hebrews 3:13. "If one has the gift of encouraging others, he should encourage" (Romans 12:8, ICB). In the Bible, we don't find phrases like "Always look for the worst in others. Back off on praise and recognition. Don't thank people too much or else they'll become proud." Quite the contrary! The early churches were oases of encouragement.

- Barnabas was called the Son of Encouragement (Acts 4:36).
- Barnabas encouraged believers in Antioch (Acts 11:23).
- Two prophets in the early church, Judas and Silas, "said much to encourage and strengthen the believers" (Acts 15:32).
- After being released from prison in Philippi, Paul and Silas went to the home of Lydia, "where they met with the brothers and sisters and encouraged them" (Acts 16:40).
- When Paul was in Macedonia, Luke wrote, "Paul sent for the disciples and, after encouraging them, said goodbye and set out for Macedonia. He traveled through that area, speaking many words of encouragement to the people" (Act 20:1-2).
- On the way to Rome, Paul the prisoner met with believers, where we read: "At the sight of these people Paul thanked God and was encouraged" (Acts 28:15).

Without question, in the first century, when people wanted to tank up on courage, confidence, and strength, they found that they could do so in the fellowship of believers. What happened in the first century can be a lifeline in our churches today.

Every day, we have many conversations in which things are said to us or we say things to others. Is what we say to others life-giving or gift-activating? One thing we can do is monitor the content of our conversations with others. We can use what I call an "Encouragement Meter."

When we often see good things in people, our default mechanism is to say nothing. It's like a well-known German saying: "Not to criticize is praise enough." Good work is expected in German society; no need to call attention to it when it happens. But this is not the Jesus way.

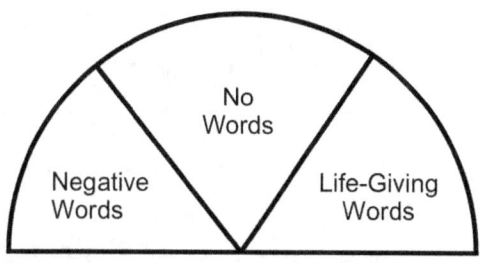

ENCOURAGEMENT METER

Figure 18. Encouragement Meter

As we become more mindful of what we say to people, we will consciously choose to live with words of affirmation and grace.

As a young seminary student, I was eager to learn from the best professors the evangelical world had to offer. Taking courses on preaching under the legendary Dr. Lloyd Perry was like sitting at the feet of Jesus. Dr. Perry, diminutive in stature and lamed by polio during his childhood, was erudite, godly, a riveting preacher, and someone who, over the span of forty years, trained some of the best preachers in the world.

My hand would go numb after an hour of furiously taking copious notes. I will never forget the day Dr. Perry stunned me. With tears in his eyes, he said, "I would rather be a kingmaker than a king."

Dr. Perry was not just the king of preachers, but the *emperor*. He was telling us that building into the lives of other people is more important than personal success. Immediately, my mind went to Jesus' words about Himself in the Gospel of Mark: "For even the Son of Man did not come to be served, but to serve, and to give his life as a ransom for many" (Mark 10:45).

When Paul wanted to encourage the younger Timothy, he reminded him of his gifting and the responsibility he had in using his gifting. Timothy was told to "stir up the gift of God which is in you" (2 Timothy 1:6, NKJV). Like with a fire that has died down to embers, Timothy was to fan the flame and bring it back to glowing again.

There are many around us like Timothy. They have gifting in them, but it has gone dormant. What leads to the nonuse of spiritual strengths is a combination of neglect and the heart erosion that comes with not taking risks for the advancement of God's cause. When this happens, listlessness and timidity invade a believer's heart. Humble leaders draw attention to the gifts that God has placed in the hearts of young leaders. Spiritual gifts are brought to a warm, burning fire by using them. Mature leaders provide young leaders with opportunities for them to fan the flame of their gifting.

Dave Ferguson's ICNU is a great starting place. ICNU means "I see in you"[2]—this strength, that character quality, this effect of your service on others. When we tell people what we see resident in them, they often rise to the occasion. When we share with others what we see in them, we can then present a challenge like "In what ways can you live out what God has deposited within you?"

I was a young Christ follower when, at the age of sixteen, a youth pastor approached me with an invitation. He said, "Dietrich, I would like you to conduct a devotional on a Wednesday morning at 6 a.m. at a breakfast for high school students." My response was, "Great! But what is a devotional?" He told me what that was and how I could prepare a fifteen-minute talk. I had not done anything like this before. I prepared the best I could, and, on a cold October morning, jumped on my motorcycle and did the devotional. Afterward, two people that I highly admired came up to me, and both of them said the same thing: "Dietrich, do you know God has given you the gift of teaching?" My response was, "Great! But what is the gift of teaching?" I did not know it at the time, but I was in a greenhouse of discipleship culture. Leaders were constantly inviting and challenging young people like me to do things they had never done before and, in the process, discover what God was doing. Eighty percent of what I learned in becoming a church planter in Germany, I learned as a teenager in my local church.

When he was still a small boy, Benjamin West, who became one of America's greatest landscape artists, decided to draw a picture of his sister. Once he had found the ink pen and the little bottle of black ink, he went to work. In the process, he proceeded to make a smearing mess of things. His mother came home from a trip and discovered the chaos on her desk. But instead of scolding him, she picked up the drawing and, looking at it closely, said, "Why, it's Sally! [What a beautiful picture of your sister!]" and kissed him. Many years later, Benjamin West recalled, "My mother's kiss made me a painter."[3]

God is calling you to kiss awake the gifts that He has placed in people around you. How can you live out your calling?

Start by making your own personal "kiss list." Write down the names of fifty people you know. Next to their names, prayerfully note their strengths, gifts, or talents. Next to their strengths, write out a short statement of affirmation that you intend to both verbalize and publicize (via a written note or email).

Name	Strengths	Affirmation Statement	
		Verbal	Writings

MY "KISS LIST"

Figure 19. My "Kiss List"

If you can say it, you can write it. If you have written it, it becomes a memorial of affirmation. A memorial of affirmation becomes a treasure stored up in the heart. The treasure in the heart becomes a burning desire. A burning desire finds its outlet in service to God and others. Humble Jesus follower, you are called to be a kingmaker. People all around you need the affirmation that only you can give because you see their strengths. Let what is seen become verbalized. Raise an army of young Jesus followers who are fed by your words of affirmation.

Growing humble followers of Jesus takes three things: an invitation to serve, a challenge to stretch beyond oneself, and a short assessment of someone seen in action.

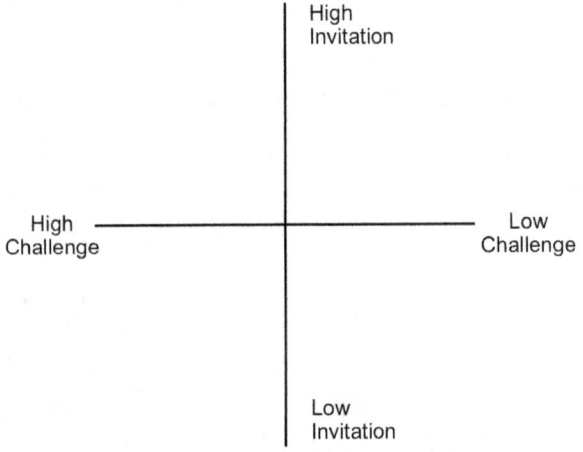

BUILDING A KINGDOM CULTURE

Figure 20. Building a Kingdom Culture

The upper left quadrant is where we want to be—high invitation coupled with high challenge. Many church ministries, however, are in one of the other quadrants. The upper right-hand quadrant—high invitation but low challenge—is the friendly church. People are invited warmly, but the implicit message is "Come as you are and stay as you are." This would be a sit-and-soak, consumer-based church.

The lower right-hand quadrant is low invitation and low challenge. In Europe, these would reflect the state churches. The onus is on the parishioner, not on the leadership. A parochial system supplants everyone as a minister with paid staff.

And lastly, the bottom left-side quadrant is high challenge paired with low invitation. In this church culture, the leadership is largely authoritarian, telling people what to do and having them report back after they have done it.

As followers of King Jesus, we are kingdom spies. We are constantly on the lookout for people, often young people, whom we can invite and challenge to do something new.

When Jan and I were planting a church in the city of Mannheim, Germany, I had a printer generate five hundred postcards. Each card had on its front side the phrase "Das war einfach Spitze!" ("That was simply first rate!" or "That was just great!") I loved catching the people in my church doing ministry well. First, I saw them in action; then I wrote them a note, telling them how wonderful they were and what they did that caught my eye. I was often surprised at how much such a simple word of encouragement meant to folks.

When we look at how Jesus trained His disciples, it becomes obvious that He was not asking for volunteers. He was rather unabashedly challenging people to follow Him. We need to do the same.

But where to start? What are the ground rules when wanting to raise leaders? We look for three seminal qualities in a person's life, as evidenced by their behavior. They need to be FAT: faithful, available, and teachable. All three qualities are needed.

Prayer is always the starting point. We discover future kingdom leaders by asking the Lord of the harvest to give them to us. This was the way of Jesus in Matthew 9:38, "Ask the Lord of the harvest, therefore, to send out workers into his harvest field." As we ask expectantly, determinedly in faith, we will receive. They are already there. Then it is good to realize that the humble followers of Christ we are looking for are already there! They do not appear out of thin air. They are right before us. Like the crowds to which Jesus spoke, most did not know that the kingdom of God and the King of the kingdom of God were right here among them. So too with those who go low, put Jesus on display, and offer this crazy world we live in a beautiful alternative to hubristic living.

Our success in life is to see others succeed. We will pray to have eyes to see them. And when we see them, we will use words to encourage them. And when we have told them ICNU—what we see in them— we will come alongside them and, like Kathy, who encouraged her one-legged father not to give up while climbing Mount Ranier, encourage them to continue following Jesus in all humility and with joy.

Those full of themselves will be stunned by the beauty of seeing humble followers of Jesus living a contrarian life, looking so much like Jesus. Many will want to follow Him, too.

Going Deeper

Questions are *quests* toward deeper insight and better application. Individually or as a group, the following questions invite you to wade into greater depth of understanding.

- Where have you recently done something new that you have never done before?
- Look at "The Encouragement Meter" (figure 18). Percentage-wise, how does your speech correlate with the three levels of encouragement (negative words, no words, life-giving words)?
- How are you celebrating the lives of other people?
- If you were to be a kingmaker and not a king, what would that look like?
- What is one truth in this chapter that you want to especially apply to your life?

Conclusion

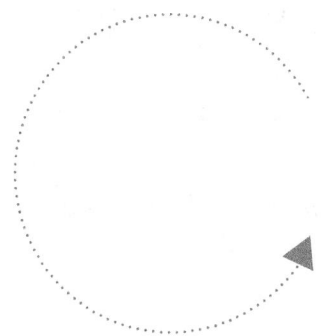

In responding to the call to follow Jesus, we are invited to learn Jesus. Learning Jesus means more than learning about Jesus or learning from Jesus. Learning Jesus is about altering our lifestyle to mirror that of our Lord. In addition to His great strength, what made Him irresistible to so many people was that He was gentle and lowly.

When people look at the way we live, they have a unique opportunity to see Jesus in us. What clouds Jesus is the self-absorbed life, the person who has a high estimation of herself coupled with a low estimation of others and God. Pride will take all that is beautiful and life-giving and will reduce it to the tawdry—the cheap and dirty.

I invite you to live a contrarian life, one that bucks the status quo and goes low to show forth the glory of God. I invite you to be a person blessed by God in mirroring Jesus with uncommon humility.

Blessed are those who relinquish the drive to strive, wanting the good life to make them feel alive.

Blessed are those who can take it lying down because they follow the One with the thorny crown.

Blessed are the looked down upon, the laughed at, the spat on, the ratted on.

175

Blessed are the upside-downers who count greatness in the elevation of others.

Blessed are the ones who serve, for God will give to them what they deserve.

Blessed are the selfless ones, who see no loss in giving away their funds.

Blessed are those who meet both friend and foe with the power to *go low*.

Endnotes

Introduction

1. D. Elton Trueblood, *Philosophy of Religion* (Grand Rapids: Baker Books, 1979), 26.
2. Saint Augustine, *Confessions* (London: Penguin Books, 1961), 93.

Chapter 1

1. F. Scott Fitzgerald, *The Great Gatsby* (London: Random House, 1925), 33.
2. Cornelius Plantinga Jr., *Not the Way It's Supposed to Be: A Breviary of Sin* (Grand Rapids: Eerdmans, 1995), 17.
3. Plantinga, *Not the Way*, 13.
4. Lewis Smedes, *Love Within Limits: A Realist's View of 1 Corinthians 13* (Grand Rapids: Eerdmans, 1978), 63–64.
5. Matt Jenson, "The Gravity of Sin: Augustine, Luther and Barth on 'Home Incurvatus in Se,'" *Themelios* 34, no. 2, accessed June 30, 2024, https://www.thegospelcoalition.org/themelios/review/the-gravity-of-sin-augustine-luther-and-barth-on-homo-incurvatus-in-se/
6. "30 Lying Statistics and Facts: How Often Do People Like?" *Golden Steps ABA*, July 28, 2023, https://www.goldenstepsaba.com/resources/lying-statistics
7. Saint Augustine, *Confessions* (London: Penguin Books, 1961), 2.2, 43–44.
8. Diane Sawyer, "Bruce Jenner: The Interview," *ABC News*, April 24, 2015, https://abcnews.go.com/2020/fullpage/bruce-jenner-the-interview-30471558.
9. Carl R. Trueman, *The Rise and Triumph of the Modern Self: Cultural Amnesia, Expressive Individualism, and the Road to Sexual Revolution* (Wheaton: Crossway, 2020), 363.
10. Fitzgerald, *The Great Gatsby*, 121.
11. Fitzgerald, *The Great Gatsby*, 148.

Chapter 2

1. Wallace Stegner, *Angle of Repose* (New York: Vintage Books, 2014), 490.
2. Barbara Mandrell, "How Can It Be Wrong (When It Feels So Right)," track 8 on *A Perfect Match*, Legacy Recordings, 1972, CD.
3. Warren I. Susman, *Culture as History: The Transformation of American Society in the Twentieth Century* (New York: Pantheon Books, 1984), 273-74.
4. Susman, *Culture as History*, 277.
5. David F. Wells, *Losing Our Virtue: Why the Church Must Recover Its Moral Vision* (Grand Rapids: Eerdmans, 1998), 97.

6. Cornelius Plantinga Jr., *Not the Way It's Supposed to Be: A Breviary of Sin* (Grand Rapids: Eerdmans, 1995), 83.

7. Oprah Winfrey, "The Greatest Discovery of Oprah's Life: What I Know for Sure" Oprah.com, accessed June 14, 2023, https://www.oprah.com/spirit/the-greatest-discovery-of-oprahs-life.

8. Wells, *Losing Our Virtue*, 126.

9. Plantinga, *Not the Way*, 125.

10. Ilya Pozin, "The Secret to Happiness? Spend Money on Experiences, Not Things," *Forbes*, March 3, 2016, https://www.forbes.com/sites/ilyapozin/2016/03/03/the-secret-to-happiness-spend-money-on-experiences-not-things/.

11. *Wall Street*, directed by Oliver Stone, 1987.

12. Barbara O'Neill, "Affluenza: The All-Consuming Epidemic," 2nd ed., *Journal of Financial Counseling & Planning* 19, no. 1 (2008): 70.

13. Dietrich Schindler, *Profound: Twelve Questions That Will Grab Your Heart and Not Let Go* (Bloomington, IN: Westbow Press, 2017), 139-141.

14. W. H. Auden, "September 1, 1939," *Another Time* (New York: Random House, 1940), https://poets.org/poem/september-1-1939.

15. Richard Dawkins, *The God Delusion* (London: Bantam Press, 2006).

16. David F. Wells, *No Place for Truth: Or, Whatever Happened to Evangelical Theology?* (Grand Rapids: Eerdmans Publishing Company, 1993), 10.

17. Jason Lehman, "Present Tense," *Dear Abby*, 1989.

Chapter 3

1. Elie Wiesel, *Night*, trans. Marion Wiesel (New York: Hill and Wang, 1958), 103.

2. Wiesel, *Night*, XIX.

3. John Stott, *The Cross of Christ* (Downers Grove: InterVarsity Press, 1986), 79.

4. C. S. Lewis, *Mere Christianity* (San Francisco: HarperCollins Publishers, 2001), 31.

5. J. I. Packer, *Knowing God* (Downers Grove: InterVarsity Press, 1973), 187–188.

6. Cornelius Plantinga Jr., *Not the Way It's Supposed to Be: A Breviary of Sin* (Grand Rapids: Eerdmans, 1995), 13.

7. Saint Augustine, *Confessions*, vol. II (London: Penguin Books, 1961), 6, 49.

8. William Manchester, *American Caesar* (Boston: Little, Brown and Company, 1978), 145, 3.

9. Plantinga, *Not the Way*, 86.

10. C. S. Lewis, *The Joyful Christian: 127 Readings from C. S. Lewis* (New York: Macmillan, 1977), 224.

11. Peter Kreeft and Ronald K. Tacelli, *Handbook of Christian Apologetics* (Downers Grove: InterVarsity Press, 1994), 282.

Section 2

1. Andrew Murray, Humility: The Journey Toward Holiness (Minneapolis: Bethany House, 2001), 34.

Chapter 4

1. Saint Augustine, Confessions (London: Penguin Books, 1961).
2. Anne Somerset, The Affair of the Poisons: Murder, Infanticide, and Satanism at the Court of Louis XIV (New York: St. Martin's Press, 2003), 62–63.
3. Kenneth S. Wuest, Philippians (Grand Rapids: Eerdmans, 1942), 70.
4. PaulVK "Dallas Willard on Not Having to Have the Last Word," Leading church. com, February 4, 2017, https://paulvanderklay.me/2017/02/04/dallas-willard-on-not-having-to-have-the-last-word/.

Chapter 5

1. James Bryan Smith, Rich Mullins: An Arrow Pointing to Heaven (Downers Grove: InterVarsity Press, 2000), 120.
2. Robertson McQuilkin, A Promise Kept: The Story of an Unforgettable Love (Wheaton: Tyndale House Publishers, 1998), 22–23.
3. McQuilkin, A Promise Kept, 85.
4. Derek Kidner, Proverbs (Downers Grove: InterVarsity Press Academic, 1964), 64.
5. John Stott, The Cross of Christ. (Downers Grove: InterVarsity Press, 1986), 73.
6. J. I. Packer and Loren Wilkinson, eds., Alive to God: Studies in Spirituality (Downers Grove: InterVarsity Press, 1992), 118.
7. Dylan Thomas, "Do Not Go Gentle into That Good Night," The Poems of Dylan Thomas (New York: New Directions, 1952), accessed July 2, 2024. https://poets.org/poem/do-not-go-gentle-good-night,
8. Dietrich Schindler, Profound: Twelve Questions That Will Grab Your Heart and Not Let Go (Bloomington, IN: Westbow Press, 2017), 119.
9. "The 23rd Psalm, Fahan Presbyterian Church, accessed July 23, 2024,
10. https://www.fahanchurch.org/the23rdpsalm.htm.
11. Robert Plant. "Stairway to Heaven." The Song Remains the Same. Succubus Music, 1971, movie track.
12. C. S. Lewis, Mere Christianity (New York: Macmillan, 1960), 196–197.

Chapter 6

1. J. E. Hutton, History of the Moravian Church (1909).
2. "Burdened to reach slaves in the West Indies with the gospel, Johann Dober and David Nitschmann literally sold themselves into slavery from which they had a platform to share the good news of Jesus—from slave to slave."

3. Chuck Swindoll, "Coming Apart," Insight for Living Ministries, June 1, 2015, https://www.insight.org/resources/daily-devotional/individual/coming-apart.

4. Matthew S. Harmon, *The Servant of the Lord and His Servant People: Tracing a Biblical Theme Through the Canon* New Studies in Biblical Theology 54, series editor D. A. Carson. (Downers Grove: InterVarsity Press Academic, 2020), 227.

5. George Herbert, "Love (III)," in Jim Scott Orrick, *A Year with George Herbert: A Guide to Fifty-Two of His Best Loved Poems* (Eugene, OR: Wipf and Stock Publishers, 2011), 153–54.

6. Orrick, *A Year with George Herbert*, 154.

Chapter 7

1. Frank Marangos, "The Value of Encouragement," Oinos Educational Consulting, January 6, 2012, https://oinosconsulting.com/2012/01/06/the-value-of-encouragement/.

2. Lee Heyward, "Interview with Stuart Briscoe," Elmbrook Church, January 2, 2022, https://www.elmbrook.org/media/sermons/interview-with-stuart-briscoe/.

Chapter 8

1. D. Martyn Lloyd-Jones, *Spiritual Depression: Its Causes and Cure* (Grand Rapids: Eerdmans, 1965), 280.

Chapter 9

1. John Steinbeck, *Travels with Charley: In Search of America* (New York: Bantam Books, 1962), 156.

2. Blaise Pascal, *Thoughts, Letters, and Minor Works*, The Harvard Classics, vol. 48, ed. Charles W. Eliot (New York: P. F. Collier & Son, 1910), 186.

3. "Pascal's Memorial" CCEL.org, accessed July 4, 2024, https://www.ccel.org/ccel/pascal/memorial.i.html.

4. Warren Wiersbe, *Real Worship: It Will Transform Your Life* (Nashville: Thomas Nelson Books, 1990), 22.

5. Martin Luther, *Small Catechism* (Saint Louis: Concordia Publishing House, 1965), 5.

Chapter 10

1. Maxwell King, *The Good Neighbor: The Life and Work of Fred Rogers* (New York: Abrams Press, 2018), 6.

2. Lewis Smedes, *Love Within Limits: A Realist's View of 1 Corinthians 13* (Grand Rapids: Eerdmans, 1978), 54.

3. John Stott, *The Cross of Christ* (Downers Grove: InterVarsity Press, 1986), 312.

4. King, *The Good Neighbor*, 21.

5. King, *The Good Neighbor*, 8.

Chapter 11

1. Plato, "The Apology of Socrates," The Center for Hellenic Studies, (38a5-6), accessed July 23, 2024, https://chs.harvard.edu/primary-source/plato-the-apology-of-socrates-sb/.
2. Barbara Lloyd, "YACHT RACING; The Yacht of Missing Solo Sailor Is Found," *New York Times,* November 23, 1992, https://www.nytimes.com/1992/11/23/sports/yacht-racing-the-yacht-of-missing-solo-sailor-is-found.html.
3. Lewis Smedes, *Love Within Limits: A Realist's View of 1 Corinthians 13* (Grand Rapids: Eerdmans, 1978), 48.
4. Bernard of Clairvaux, Sermon 42 on Canticle 6, *The Steps of Humility* (Cambridge: Harvard University Press, 1942), 51.
5. Henri Nouwen, *Discernment: Reading the Signs of Daily Life* (New York: HarperCollins Publishers, 2015), 6.
6. Nouwen, *Discernment,* 7.
7. Nouwen, *Discernment,* 17.
8. Nouwen, *Discernment,* 17.

Chapter 12

1. C. S. Lewis, *The Weight of Glory* (San Francisco: HarperCollins Publishers, 2000), 191.
2. Henri Nouwen, *Discernment: Reading the Signs of Daily Life* (New York: HarperCollins Publishers, 2015), 51.
3. J. H. Sammis, "Trust and Obey," 1887, accessed July 8, 2024, https://www.hymnal.net/en/hymn/h/582.
4. Louisa M. R. Stead, "'Tis So Sweet to Trust in Jesus," 1882, accessed July 8, 2024, https://hymnary.org/text/tis_so_sweet_to_trust_in_jesus_just_to.
5. Dietrich Bonhoeffer, *The Cost of Discipleship,* revised ed. (New York: Macmillan, 1963; first published, 1937), 45.

Chapter 13

1. Bob Buford, Quote Fancy, accessed July 8, 2024, https://quotefancy.com/quote/1791003/Bob-Buford-My-fruit-grows-on-other-people-s-trees.
2. Dave DeSelm, "ICNU," Dave DeSelm Ministries, December 8, 2020, https://www.davedeselmministries.org/blog/icnu.
3. Don McMinn, "Mother's Kiss Made Me an Artist—The Power of Affirmation," December 3, 2019, https://donmcminn.com/2019/12/mothers-kiss-made-me-an-artist-the-power-of-affirmation/.